PRAYING
THE
Word
EFFECTIVELY

Revised and Expanded

Praying the Word Effectively

Compiled by Linda Gleason and Gwyn Oakes

© 2004 United Pentecostal Church International
Hazelwood, MO 63042-2299

Revised and Expanded 2011

ISBN 0-7577-2967-3

Designer: Laura Jurek

All Scripture quotations in this book are from the King James Version of the Bible unless otherwise identified.

Printed in the United States of America
Printed by Pentecostal Publishing House

More to Life
8855 Dunn Road
Hazelwood, MO 63042

PRAYING THE *Word* EFFECTIVELY

*Prayer is a powerful thing,
for God has bound and tied
Himself thereto. None can
believe how powerful prayer is,
and what it is able to effect,
but those who have learned it
by experience.*

MARTIN LUTHER

Table of Contents

CONTRIBUTING WRITERS

Anonymous

Andrea Arcovio

Margie Becton

Connie Bernard

Wanda Chavis

Kathy Crossley

Ethel Dibble

Beth Dillon

Linda Gleason

Marlene Gleason

Carolyn Hanson

Margaret Harden

Nancy Harrison

Brenda Hudson

Marjorie Kinnee

Mary Loudermilk

Kala Martin

Marilyn McDonald

Gwyn Oakes

Bonnie Peacock

Indira Petoskey

Peggy Readout

Melody Reever

Anne Richardson

Darie Scott

Debra Scott

Leah Seagraves

Darla Sims

Shelia Sims

Kaye Singleton

Thomas Suey

Donna Ten Eyck

Freddi Trammell

Claudette Walker

Raymond Woodward

The Power of Prayer

As I entered the room, I could hear sounds of someone who seemed to be in pain. As I drew closer, I could see the figure of a woman on her knees. She was weeping uncontrollably and groaning. On the floor beside her lie several photos of her family: her husband, her children and their spouses, and her grandchildren. She was weeping for her children.

It is time we become possessed with an overwhelming love for God and with a hatred for the enemy of our souls. The battle for our families can only be won through fervent intercessory prayer. "For the weapons of our warfare are not carnal, but mighty through God to the pulling down of strong holds" (II Corinthians 10:4).

Only through prayer can we be victorious. We can do all things through Christ which strengthens us when we pray. When we, as the children of God, unite in prayer for a common purpose, no force of the enemy can stop us. "For as soon as Zion travailed, she brought forth her children" (Isaiah 66:8). Let's do it! Let's let God arise and His enemies be scattered! Let us unite in prayer and claim the victory for our families, our country, our nation, our world!

Use this book as a guide to lead to a deeper understanding of what can be done through the power of the Word of God. Pray the Word; it is forever settled in heaven!

Gwyn Oakes
With Phyllis Smith

Affecting Our World
through Prayer

How can we affect our world? It may seem like such a daunting task, but we can make a difference. How? Through prayer. Simple prayer. Simple prayers—even a single word!—whether outwardly spoken or echoed in the heart, impact our world. You may ask, "How could my simple words make any difference?" They make all the difference when spoken in earnest to our loving and all-powerful God!

Many of us seem to think that if our prayer is not an hour long, God does not hear us. God hears every prayer His children pray, however short or long! When we merely speak His name, He is instantly attentive to our plea. There is a level of prayer that you can get to in which you do not have to stay before the throne for hours before you are certain He has heard your cry. It may only take a whisper to breathe His name before you know He is there and has heard you. Regardless of how long we pray, we can be confident that He hears us, because He loves us and desires for us to talk with Him. He has in fact commanded us to pray, and He lovingly waits for us to bring our petitions to Him.

We need set times of prayer each day, of course, but even more so we need to cultivate a mindset of prayer every day, everywhere. We are to "pray without ceasing" (I Thessalonians 5:17). We are His hands, His feet, His voice, His ears. A simple touch, a simple prayer makes such a difference to someone. A mindset of prayer prepares us to be the kind of person God can use to pray for others throughout the day.

Many times in my life I have known that I simply could not make

11

it on my own. In those times the Lord has brought my name, my need, to someone. How many of you have had a deep burden that seemed too heavy to bear and then someone called you and let you know that they were praying for you?

Many times in the past I would be going through my day and someone would come to mind seemingly out of nowhere. I used to just think, "I wonder how they are these days?" But when people are brought to our attention and we are in that mindset of prayer and are sensitive and aware of God's presence, we can be sure that God has brought that person's name to our attention for a reason. Stop and take them to the throne of God! Only He knows what the situation is at that time.

I will never forget the story that Brother Bernard told me about his father and aunt. His father was stationed in Korea during the Korean War. His sister in Louisiana was home one day washing her dishes, and her brother came to mind. She thought about him and prayed briefly. As she continued washing the dishes, she quickly realized that that was not enough. She stopped and began to intercede for him until she felt a release.

It was only later, after receiving a letter from him, that she realized God had used her to pray a prayer of protection for him. For at the very same time she had felt the burden to pray for her brother while in Louisiana, he had felt a strong urge to sit down in his tent in Korea. At the moment he sat down, a bullet whizzed through the tent at the very spot where his head would have been!

The Lord miraculously protected him that day through the prayers of his sister. What would have happened if she had not stopped to pray? What if she had disregarded the strong urge to pray? I think the Lord would have brought protection from another source, but oh, what a joy for his sister to know she had been used to intervene and intercede on her brother's behalf and God had delivered him— and what a glorious thought that the Lord can use us as well to affect our world and the lives of others when we pray!

God loves us. We are His children. He wants to bless us. He loves to hear our voice calling out to Him, talking with Him, communing with Him. It is in these times of close communion, especially as we commune with Him throughout our day, that the Lord can use us in a miraculous way to touch and strengthen someone else through our prayers.

Let's not forget the power of prayer! Whether it is a simple whispered prayer or a powerful intercessory prayer, our loving Father hears them and acts upon them. He wants nothing more than to do this. He is longing to reach out and do marvelous things for us and through us. Let's seek Him and yield to Him. Let's affect our world through prayer.

Connie Bernard

Why Pray
the Word?

---•---

You may wonder, "Why pray the Word? Won't God hear me if I just pray what I need?" Yes, He hears the cries of our heart and knows our every need even before we pray. However, God gives us a spiritual sword of power. It is His Word.

II Corinthians 10 reminds us that our weapons of warfare are not carnal, or of the world, but they are mighty through God for the pulling down of strongholds. If we want God to fight the battle for us, we need to fight it the way He directs us. We must fight with His Word. We are not fighting with our strength, but in His. The battle is the Lord's, but we are privileged to be a conduit He works through.

"In the beginning was the Word, and the Word was with God, and the Word was God" (John 1:1).

So the Word of God is God? Exactly. From Genesis, when God simply spoke the world into existence, to Revelation, where God will conquer and judge in perfect truth, God is the Word. If we want God in the middle of our circumstances, we must pray the Word into our circumstances. He is the sovereign God and nothing shall stand against Him. We have the Conqueror on our side.

"So shall my word be that goeth forth out of my mouth: it shall not return unto me void, but it shall accomplish that which I please, and it shall prosper in the thing whereto I sent it" (Isaiah 55:11).

Focused Prayer
for Our
Children

It is time to take decisive action against the encroachment of evil. The enemy has targeted our children for destruction, but we must not sit idly by. We have the power and authority by the Word of God, the name of Jesus, and the blood of the Lamb. That authority coupled with the compelling power of love is a combination that is unbeatable and will overcome any tactic of Satan.

We invite you to join with us as we invade the enemy's territory, tear down strongholds, take back what belongs to us, and preserve the next generation for the kingdom of God. Through the power of prayer, Satan will be driven back. Together let us lift up our hands to the Lord for the lives of our children.

"But the mercy of the Lord is from everlasting to everlasting
On those who fear Him,
And His righteousness to children's children,
To such as keep His covenant,
And to those who remember His commandments to do them"
(Psalm 103:17-18, NKJV).

"For this child I prayed, and the Lord has granted me my petition which I asked of Him. Therefore I also have lent him to the Lord; as long as he lives he shall be lent to the Lord"
(I Samuel 1:27-28, NKJV).

"All the Christian virtues are locked up in the word 'prayer.'"
Charles Spurgeon

Praying the Word
for Your Children

Parents do well in attempting to pass the virtues of Christian living on to their children. However, if they fail to strengthen their teaching with prayer, they may become frustrated and miserably disappointed with their efforts.

Praying for your child involves petitioning God for His input into the fiber of your child's everyday life. God hears the sincere and fervent prayers of parents. This fact is proven from examples in the Scriptures. Jarius sought diligently for Jesus when his little daughter lie dying, and Jesus raised her up. The Shunammite woman persisted until her house and land were restored for her and her son. Rizpah passionately persevered for her sons and for the grandchildren of Saul whom she raised, until the king heard and answered her plea.

There is a God-given desire in the heart of every child to know Him. Nurture this desire in your children with fervent prayer and encouraging words. It can lead children into a lifetime of meaningful relationship with God. Be proactive and not reactive; pray for them from birth that they will love and serve the Lord. Never wait until the problems of life arise to pray for those situations that may come.

My son-in-law lifted his newborn son up toward heaven and prayed: "Hear, O Israel: The LORD our God is one LORD: and thou shalt love the LORD thy God with all thine heart, and with all thy soul, and with all thy might" (Deuteronomy 6:4). The Jewish doctor in attendance was so affected by this that he draped his arm over Jonathan's shoulders and wept. It was later found that the baby's left hand

and fingers lie limp with no movement. We prayed the verse of Scripture concerning the man with the withered hand. Jesus told him to stretch forth his hand. When he obeyed, the crippled hand became whole. We prayed: "This hand will become whole as the other, in Jesus' name!" ... and it did!

A mother who was disturbed that her son's name was at the bottom of the academic list in his class began to pray. Placing her son's name in a verse of Scripture she said, "The Lord shall make *Jeremy* the head and not the tail; and *Jeremy* shall be above only, and *Jeremy* shall not be beneath" (Deuteronomy 28:13). She prayed this verse of Scripture for her son earnestly and fervently. She believed that by the help of the Lord her son's name would soon head the academic list in his class. The next time she went to the classroom, posted on the door was the list of the students' current academic level. Jeremy's name was the first one on the list!

Praying the Word of God is far from passive praying. Jesus said, "When you seek me with your whole heart, then I will be found."

My mother-in-law was a woman of prayer. Every morning and evening she called each child's name in prayer. She never allowed any kind of circumstance, including visiting relatives, illness, nor household chores, to stop her daily prayers. She prevailed over the enemy for her household. As they married, she added their companion's name, then each grandchild's name, to her list. She prayed, not for riches and worldly honor, but with simple, sincere words that the Lord would save her children. As a result, many of them are preachers of the gospel and workers in God's kingdom. When it is evident that a parent values prayer and the Word of God, this faith and practice is more likely to also become a way of life for the child.

Spirit-filled parents who believe in and love the Word of God are equipped to pray prevailing prayers for their children. Through prayer, parents receive wisdom to guide their children in godly lifestyles.

"Their heart cried unto the Lord, O wall of the daughter of Zion, let tears run down like a river day and night: give thyself no rest; let not the apple of thine eye cease. Arise, cry out in the night: in the beginning of the watches pour out thine heart like water before the face of the Lord: lift up thy hands toward him for the life of thy young children, that faint for hunger in the top of every street" (Lamentations 2:18-19).

Faith and prayer will overcome Satan's ploy to destroy your child. Nothing can take the place of persistent, consistent prayer. Praying the Word of God is the most powerful method of prayer: "For the word of God is quick, and powerful, and sharper than any twoedged sword, piercing even to the dividing asunder of soul and spirit, and of the joints and marrow, and is a discerner of the thoughts and intents of the heart" (Hebrews 4:12).

Learn to pray the Scriptures relative to what is happening in your child's life. Pray positively! Establish Scripture in your heart for prayer. When emergency situations arise, you can pray the Word of God with confidence and with power. We are admonished to let the Word "dwell in you richly" (Colossians 3:16).

I received a call that my daughter was injured in an accident. As I raced through the house to leave for the emergency room, I flipped open the Bible lying on the table. This verse of Scripture leaped from the page: "For He shall give his angels charge over thee ... They shall bear thee up in their hands, lest thou dash thy foot against a stone" (Psalm 91:11-12). I immediately began to pray these words. God intervened and my daughter was saved.

On page 20 I have given you two verses of Scripture as examples of praying the Word for your child. Look them up in the Bible and compare the wording. As you study, you will find many, many more. Boldly proclaim them before the throne of God with your child's name interjected in them.

- **Psalm 119:114:** "Be my child's hiding place and his shield; let him hope in Thy Word, oh Lord."

- **Psalm 27:1-3:** "Be my child's light and his salvation; whom shall he fear? Be the strength of his life, oh Lord, then of whom shall he be afraid? When the wicked, even his enemies and his foes, come upon him, let them stumble and fall. Though a host should camp against him, let not his heart fear; though war should rise against him, let him be confident in You, Lord."

There is no greater power than God's Word. As you read the Word, you will find an abundance of Scripture verses that you can pray for any situation.

Your Child's Salvation

Acts 2:38-39

"Then Peter said unto them, Repent, and be baptized every one of you in the name of Jesus Christ for the remission of sins, and ye shall receive the gift of the Holy Ghost. For the promise is unto you, and to your children, and to all that are afar off, even as many as the Lord our God shall call."

Psalm 18:2

"The LORD is my rock, and my fortress, and my deliverer; my God, my strength, in whom I will trust; my buckler, and the horn of my salvation, and my high tower."

Pray this:

Be my child's rock, his fortress, his deliverance, and his strength. Help him trust in You; be his buckler, his salvation, and his strong tower.

Psalm 20:5-6

"We will rejoice in thy salvation, and in the name of our God we will set up our banners: the LORD fulfil all thy petitions. Now know I that the LORD saveth his anointed; he will hear him from his holy heaven with the saving strength of his right hand."

Psalm 24:4-5

"He that hath clean hands, and a pure heart; who hath not lifted up his soul unto vanity, nor sworn deceitfully. He shall receive the blessing from the LORD, and righteousness from the God of his salvation."

Psalm 25:4-7

"Shew me thy ways, O LORD; teach me thy paths. Lead me in thy truth, and teach me: for thou art the God of my salvation; on thee do I wait all the day. Remember, O LORD, thy tender mercies and thy lovingkindnesses; for they have been ever of old. Remember not the sins of my youth, nor my transgressions: according to thy mercy remember thou me for thy goodness' sake, O LORD."

Psalm 27:1-4

"The LORD is my light and my salvation; whom shall I fear? the LORD is the strength of my life; of whom shall I be afraid? When the wicked, even mine enemies and my foes, came upon me to eat up my flesh, they stumbled and fell. Though an host should encamp against me, my heart shall not fear: though war should rise against me, in this will I be confident. One thing have I desired of the LORD, that will I seek after; that I may dwell in the house of the LORD all the days of my life, to behold the beauty of the LORD, and to enquire in his temple."

Psalm 62:6-7

"He only is my rock and my salvation: he is my defence; I shall not be moved. In God is my salvation and my glory: the rock of my strength, and my refuge, is in God."

Taking Ownership of the Faith at an Accountable Age

Pray that your child will take ownership of the faith at an accountable age so that it will become his faith, not just the faith of his parents.

Psalm 119:11-16

> "Thy word have I hid in mine heart, that I might not sin against thee. Blessed art thou, O LORD: teach me thy statutes. With my lips have I declared all the judgments of thy mouth. I have rejoiced in the way of thy testimonies, as much as in all riches. I will meditate in thy precepts, and have respect unto thy ways. I will delight myself in thy statutes: I will not forget thy word."

Pray the preceding verse of Scripture the following way:

Help my child to hide Your Word in his heart so that he will not sin against You, Lord. Blessed are You, Lord, for You will teach him Your statutes. Help him declare with his own lips all the judgments You have set. Help him to rejoice in the way of Your testimonies as much as he would in riches. Help him to meditate in Your precepts and have respect to Your ways. Help him delight in Your laws and not forget Your Word.

Now pray the following in the same method:

Psalm 25:5

"Lead me in thy truth, and teach me: for thou art the God of my salvation; on thee do I wait all the day."

Psalm 51:6

"Behold, thou desirest truth in the inward parts: and in the hidden part thou shalt make me to know wisdom."

Proverbs 3:3-6

"Let not mercy and truth forsake thee: bind them about thy neck; write them upon the table of thine heart: so shalt thou find favour and good understanding in the sight of God and man. Trust in the LORD with all thine heart; and lean not unto thine own understanding. In all thy ways acknowledge him, and he shall direct thy paths."

Isaiah 26:3

"Thou wilt keep him in perfect peace, whose mind is stayed on thee: because he trusteth in thee."

John 8:32

"And ye shall know the truth, and the truth shall make you free."

Additional verses you may claim:

Psalm 103:17
Proverbs 23:23-26
Matthew 15:28
Matthew 17:20
I Corinthians 16:13
II Corinthians 13:8
I Timothy 6:12
II Timothy 1:5

Health and Protection

Psalm 91:9-12

"Because thou hast made the LORD, which is my refuge, even the most High, thy habitation; there shall no evil befall thee, neither shall any plague come nigh thy dwelling. For he shall give his angels charge over thee, to keep thee in all thy ways. They shall bear thee up in their hands, lest thou dash thy foot against a stone."

Pray this:

Dear Lord, please help my child to make You his refuge, his very habitation. Your Word promises that if he does, it is not likely that evil will snare him nor any plagues come near his home. Give Your angels charge over him to keep him in all Your ways—not just part, but all your ways Lord. Let the angels bear him up in their hands, oh Lord, and keep him from harm.

Continue by praying the following verses and others in the same manner:

Deuteronomy 31:8

"And the LORD, he it is that doth go before thee; he will be with thee, he will not fail thee, neither forsake thee: fear not, neither be dismayed."

Psalm 3:3

"But thou, O Lord, art a shield for me; my glory, and the lifter up of mine head."

Psalm 17:8

"Keep me as the apple of the eye, hide me under the shadow of thy wings."

Psalm 34:17

"The righteous cry, and the Lord heareth, and delivereth them out of all their troubles."

Psalm 63:7

"Because thou hast been my help, therefore in the shadow of thy wings will I rejoice."

Psalm 121:7-8

"The Lord shall preserve thee from all evil: he shall preserve thy soul. The Lord shall preserve thy going out and thy coming in from this time forth, and even for evermore."

Proverbs 3:23

"Then shalt thou walk in thy way safely, and thy foot shall not stumble."

Additional verses you may claim:

Deuteronomy 33:27
Exodus 15:26
Exodus 22:22-23
Psalm 23:6
Proverbs 14:26
Proverbs 18:10
Proverbs 22:6
Isaiah 40:31
Matthew 19:14
II Corinthians 12:9

Choosing Friends

II Corinthians 6:14

"Be ye not unequally yoked together with unbelievers: for what fellowship [friendship] hath righteousness with unrighteousness?"

Help my child to not only apply this verse of Scripture to marriage but also to friends and business partners.

Ephesians 5:11

"And have no fellowship with the unfruitful works of darkness, but rather reprove them."

Help him to stay away from the works of evil and darkness and to stand against them coming into his lifestyle.

Ephesians 6:1

"Children, obey your parents in the Lord."

Help my child to understand that this commandment is meant for his own good and protection, and that it is the God-given responsibility of children to obey and respect parents.

Good Choices

I Samuel 18:1

"The soul of Jonathan was knit with the soul of David, and Jonathan loved him as his own soul."

Help my child to study Your Word to find good examples of choosing the right friends.

II Timothy 1:5

"When I [Paul] call to remembrance the unfeigned faith that is in thee, which dwelt first in thy grandmother Lois, and thy mother Eunice, and I am persuaded that in thee also."

Help my child to realize that there is knowledge and discernment in mothers and grandmothers who have gleaned wisdom through the years, and that they do offer good advice in life's choices.

Bad Choices

II Kings 2:23-24

"As he [Elijah] was going up by the way, there came forth little children ... and mocked him, and said unto him, Go up, thou bald head; go up, thou bald head. ... And he turned back, and looked on them, and cursed them ... And there came forth two she bears out of the wood, and tare forty and two children of them."

Judges 13:24-25

"And the woman bare a son, and called his name Samson: and the child grew, and the Lᴏʀᴅ blessed him. And the Spirit of the Lᴏʀᴅ began to move him at times in the camp of Dan between Zorah and Eshtaol."

Samson had a good start in obeying the Lord, but changed as he grew older. Pray that your child will see the end of those who leave God out of the plans for their lives.

Judges 16:30

"And Samson said, Let me die with the Philistines. And he bowed himself with all his might; and the house fell upon the lords, and upon all the people that were therein. So the dead which he slew at his death were more than they which he slew in his life."

Samson began with the Spirit of the Lord. His choice of friends resulted in a broken relationship with his parents as well as with God. Ultimately, it cost his life!

Moral
Purity

I Peter 1:13-16

> "Wherefore gird up the loins of your mind, be sober, and hope to the end for the grace that is to be brought unto you at the revelation of Jesus Christ; as obedient children, not fashioning yourselves according to the former lusts in your ignorance: but as he which hath called you is holy, so be ye holy in all manner of conversation; because it is written, Be ye holy; for I am holy."

Pray this powerful passage in the following manner:

Dear Lord, help my child to bring his mind in subjection to You. Let him be sober in all things. Keep eternal hope of the revelation of who You are alive in his heart and mind. Never let it slip! Help him to do this unto You as an obedient child would honor his parent. Don't ever let him turn to the lusts of the flesh as an ignorant person, but cling to Your ways as a wise person does. Stir his mind to remember that because You are holy, he must also be holy in his appearance as well as in his heart. Help him to realize that what is written in Your Word are the words of life, and they will help us to find Your will for our lives.

Continue the same format with the following verses:

Matthew 5:8

"Blessed are the pure in heart: for they shall see God."

Galatians 5:16

"This I say then, Walk in the Spirit, and ye shall not fulfil the lust of the flesh."

Ephesians 4:22-24

"That ye put off concerning the former conversation the old man, which is corrupt according to the deceitful lusts; and be renewed in the spirit of your mind; and that ye put on the new man, which after God is created in righteousness and true holiness."

Philippians 4:8

"Finally, brethren, whatsoever things are true, whatsoever things are honest, whatsoever things are just, whatsoever things are pure, whatsoever things are lovely, whatsoever things are of good report; if there be any virtue, and if there be any praise, think on these things."

I Timothy 4:12

"Let no man despise thy youth; but be thou an example of the believers, in word, in conversation, in charity, in spirit, in faith, in purity."

I Timothy 5:22

"Lay hands suddenly on no man, neither be partaker of other men's sins: keep thyself pure."

II Timothy 2:22

"Flee also youthful lusts: but follow righteousness, faith, charity, peace, with them that call on the Lord out of a pure heart."

Titus 2:11-12

"For the grace of God that bringeth salvation hath appeared to all men, teaching us that, denying ungodliness and worldly lusts, we should live soberly, righteously, and godly, in this present world."

James 1:21-22

"Wherefore lay apart all filthiness and superfluity of naughtiness, and receive with meekness the engrafted word, which is able to save your souls. But be ye doers of the word, and not hearers only, deceiving your own selves."

I Peter 2:11

"Dearly beloved, I beseech you as strangers and pilgrims, abstain from fleshly lusts, which war against the soul."

I John 2:17

"And the world passeth away, and the lust thereof: but he that doeth the will of God abideth for ever."

Spiritual Discernment

Psalm 25:4-5

"Shew me thy ways, O Lord; teach me thy paths. Lead me in thy truth, and teach me: for thou art the God of my salvation; on thee do I wait all the day."

Pray this:

Show my child Your ways, Lord. Teach him the paths he should follow. Lead him in Thy truth and teach him continually. You are the only God of his salvation, so help him to always wait on you for direction and discernment of right and wrong.

Psalm 32:8

"I will instruct thee and teach thee in the way which thou shalt go: I will guide thee with mine eye."

Psalm 37:23

"The steps of a good man are ordered by the Lord: and he delighteth in his way."

Psalm 119:105

"Thy word is a lamp unto my feet, and a light unto my path."

Psalm 143:10

"Teach me to do thy will; for thou art my God: thy spirit is good; lead me into the land of uprightness."

Proverbs 3:4-5

"So shalt thou find favour and good understanding in the sight of God and man. Trust in the Lord with all thine heart; and lean not unto thine own understanding."

Proverbs 12:15

"The way of a fool is right in his own eyes: but he that hearkeneth unto counsel is wise."

Isaiah 30:21

"And thine ears shall hear a word behind thee, saying, This is the way, walk ye in it, when ye turn to the right hand, and when ye turn to the left."

Isaiah 48:17

"Thus saith the Lord, thy Redeemer, the Holy One of Israel; I am the Lord thy God which teacheth thee to profit, which leadeth thee by the way that thou shouldest go."

Isaiah 7:15

"Butter and honey shall he eat, that he may know to refuse the evil, and choose the good."

John 10:3-4

"To him the porter openeth; and the sheep hear his voice: and he calleth his own sheep by name, and leadeth them out. And when he putteth forth his own sheep, he goeth before them, and the sheep follow him: for they know his voice."

Acts 22:14

"And he said, The God of our fathers hath chosen thee, that thou shouldest know his will, and see that Just One, and shouldest hear the voice of his mouth."

I Corinthians 2:14

"But the natural man receiveth not the things of the Spirit of God: for they are foolishness unto him: neither can he know them, because they are spiritually discerned."

II Thessalonians 3:3

"But the Lord is faithful, who shall stablish you, and keep you from evil."

Future Career

Career Choices

Heavenly Father, thank You for giving my child direction regarding the career he will choose. Order his steps and place Your desires in his heart. Thank You for the plan You have for my child's life to prosper her, a plan of hope and a good future. Open the eyes of her understanding and show her Your good and perfect will for her life. Give him revelation and understanding about what to do! Give him a clear understanding and a singleness of mind, for You are not the author of confusion. Let her mind be alert and her heart be receptive in Your mighty name. Thank You, Father, for preparing my child for such a time as this. And Lord, as he steps into his career, thank You for opening up effective doors of opportunity for him today.

Pray the following verses of Scripture as a promise from the Lord:

Esther 4:14

"For if thou altogether holdest thy peace at this time, then shall there enlargement and deliverance arise to the Jews from another place; but thou and thy father's house shall be destroyed: and who knoweth whether thou art come to the kingdom for such a time as this?"

Psalm 5:12

"For thou, LORD, wilt bless the righteous; with favour wilt thou compass him as with a shield."

Psalm 37:23

"The steps of a good man are ordered by the LORD: and he delighteth in his way."

Jeremiah 29:11

"For I know the thoughts that I think toward you, saith the LORD, thoughts of peace, and not of evil, to give you an expected end."

Romans 12:2

"And be not conformed to this world: but be ye transformed by the renewing of your mind, that ye may prove what is that good, and acceptable, and perfect, will of God."

I Corinthians 14:33

"For God is not the author of confusion, but of peace, as in all churches of the saints."

I Corinthians 16:9

"For a great door and effectual is opened unto me, and there are many adversaries."

● Preparing for the Future

Heavenly Father, I come before You today to praise You for my child. Help him take the right steps as he prepares for the future. Thank You that You are the One who is ordering his steps and leading and guiding him in the way he should go. I pray that he will listen to Your voice and obey it. I ask that he will prepare for the future by spending time in Your Word and in prayer. Just as our feet are shod with the preparation of the gospel of peace, so prepare my child's spirit, soul, and body for the task You have laid before him. Thank You for guiding him with Your counsel. You are his rock and fortress, the One who leads and guides him into all truth. My child is more than a conqueror, with victory and success in his future! In the name of Jesus. Amen.

Pray the following as promises for the future:

Deuteronomy 10:12

"And now, Israel, what doth the LORD thy God require of thee, but to fear the LORD thy God, to walk in all his ways, and to love him, and to serve the LORD thy God with all thy heart and with all thy soul."

I Chronicles 28:9

"And thou, Solomon my son, know thou the God of thy father, and serve him with a perfect heart and with a willing mind: for the LORD searcheth all hearts, and understandeth all the imaginations of the thoughts: if thou seek him, he will be found of thee; but if thou forsake him, he will cast thee off for ever."

Psalm 31:3

"For thou art my rock and my fortress; therefore for thy name's sake lead me, and guide me."

Proverbs 16:3

"Commit thy works unto the LORD, and thy thoughts shall be established."

Micah 6:8

"He hath shewed thee, O man, what is good; and what doth the LORD require of thee, but to do justly, and to love mercy, and to walk humbly with thy God?"

Romans 12:11

"Not slothful in business; fervent in spirit; serving the Lord."

I Corinthians 4:2

"Moreover it is required in stewards, that a man be found faithful."

Philippians 4:13

"I can do all things through Christ which strengtheneth me."

Colossians 3:22-23

"Servants, obey in all things your masters according to the flesh; not with eyeservice, as menpleasers; but in singleness of heart, fearing God: and whatsoever ye do, do it heartily, as to the Lord, and not unto men."

Pray the following verses in the same manner:

Deuteronomy 5:27
Psalm 73:24
Proverbs 24:27
Romans 8:37
Ephesians 6:15

Finding the Will
of God

Matthew 6:33
> "But seek ye first the kingdom of God, and his righteousness; and all these things shall be added unto you."

Pray the preceding verse this way:

Lord, help my child to always seek Your kingdom, that he would be filled with Your Spirit, and serve You righteously. Help him to understand that as his creator, You have definite plans for his life, and that when he has earnestly sought You for guidance, the things he needs to succeed will be provided. Help him to understand that the steps of a good man are ordered by the Lord.

Continue by praying the following verses and others in the same manner:

Psalm 144:12
> "That our sons may be as plants grown up in their youth; that our daughters may be as corner stones, polished after the similitude of a palace."

Proverbs 4:26
> "Ponder the path of thy feet, and let all thy ways be established."

Proverbs 16:3

"Commit thy works unto the Lᴏʀᴅ, and thy thoughts shall be established."

Proverbs 3:5-6

"Trust in the Lᴏʀᴅ with all thine heart; and lean not unto thine own understanding. In all thy ways acknowledge him, and he shall direct thy paths."

Isaiah 41:10

"Fear thou not; for I am with thee: be not dismayed; for I am thy God: I will strengthen thee; yea, I will help thee; yea, I will uphold thee with the right hand of my righteousness."

Isaiah 49:25

"But thus saith the Lᴏʀᴅ, Even the captives of the mighty shall be taken away, and the prey of the terrible shall be delivered: for I will contend with him that contendeth with thee, and I will save thy children."

Isaiah 54:17

"No weapon that is formed against thee shall prosper; and every tongue that shall rise against thee in judgment thou shalt condemn. This is the heritage of the servants of the Lᴏʀᴅ, and their righteousness is of me, saith the Lᴏʀᴅ."

Jeremiah 29:11

"For I know the thoughts that I think toward you, saith the Lᴏʀᴅ, thoughts of peace, and not of evil, to give you an expected end."

Romans 8:28

"And we know that all things work together for good to them that love God, to them who are the called according to his purpose."

Philippians 4:6

"Be careful for nothing; but in every thing by prayer and supplication with thanksgiving let your requests be made known unto God."

II Timothy 1:12

"For the which cause I also suffer these things: nevertheless I am not ashamed: for I know whom I have believed, and am persuaded that he is able to keep that which I have committed unto him against that day."

Future Spouse

Jeremiah 29:11

"For I know the thoughts that I think toward you, saith the LORD, thoughts of peace and not of evil, to give you an expected end."

Pray Jeremiah's promise the following way for your child or for yourself:

I thank You, Lord, that my child is in Your thoughts and that You have a definite plan for Your children. You said that You had thoughts of peace for my child's life as well as mine. I ask that You send the spouse You have in mind for my child, the one that will help him in his walk with You, that Your peace would rest in their home, and that Your ways would be their ways. I pray that they would look for and expect Your presence and blessing on their lives. I pray that the gospel of peace would be taught in their future and that they would bless You all their days.

Psalm 37:34

"Wait on the LORD, and keep his way, and he shall exalt thee to inherit the land."

Proverbs 4:14

"Enter not into the path of the wicked, and go not in the way of evil men."

Proverbs 16:20

"He that handleth a matter wisely shall find good: and whoso trusteth in the Lᴏʀᴅ, happy is he."

Proverbs 31:10-12

"Who can find a virtuous woman? for her price is far above rubies. The heart of her husband doth safely trust in her, so that he shall have no need of spoil. She will do him good and not evil all the days of her life."

Proverbs 31:27-28

"She looketh well to the ways of her household, and eateth not the bread of idleness. Her children arise up, and call her blessed; her husband also, and he praiseth her."

Matthew 6:33

"But seek ye first the kingdom of God, and his righteousness; and all these things shall be added unto you."

Matthew 7:7-8

"Ask, and it shall be given you; seek, and ye shall find; knock, and it shall be opened unto you: for every one that asketh receiveth; and he that seeketh findeth; and to him that knocketh it shall be opened."

Colossians 1:9-10

"For this cause we also, since the day we heard it, do not cease to pray for you, and to desire that ye might be filled with the knowledge of his will in all wisdom and spiritual understanding; that ye might walk worthy of the Lord unto all pleasing, being fruitful in every good work, and increasing in the knowledge of God."

Focused Prayer
for My
Spouse and Family

---●---

"And if it seem evil unto you to serve the LORD,
choose you this day whom ye will serve ...
but as for me and my house,
we will serve the LORD"
(Joshua 24:15).

"For I have known him, in order that he may command his
children and his household after him, that they keep the
way of the LORD, to do righteousness and justice, that the
LORD may bring to Abraham what He has spoken to him"
(Genesis 18:19, NKJV).

"My son, if thou wilt receive my words,
and hide my commandments with thee;
so that thou incline thine ear unto wisdom,
and apply thine heart to understanding;
yea, if thou criest after knowledge,
and liftest up thy voice for understanding;
if thou seekest her as silver,
and searchest for her as for hid treasures;
then shalt thou understand the fear of the LORD,
and find the knowledge of God"
(Proverbs 2:1-5).

Praying the Word
for Your Spouse

A strong biblical marriage is best described as a "threefold cord" which is not quickly broken (Ecclesiastes 4:12). God desires for our marriages to have intimacy of spirit, soul, and body. Usually couples need help most in developing spiritual intimacy. The foundation of becoming one in spirit is to pray for and with each other.

Ask your spouse what prayer requests he/she has and then record them with dates in a prayer journal. Get out your spiritual shovel and begin to dig in the goldmine of God's Word for a gold nugget of promise to cover the need. For example, if the need is financial, pray Psalm 37:25: "I have been young, and now am old; yet have I not seen the righteous forsaken, nor his seed begging bread."

Paul's prayers for the churches are powerful prayers to pray. Insert your spouse's name in Ephesians 3:14-19:

> "For this cause I bow my knees unto the Father of our Lord Jesus Christ, of whom the whole family in heaven and earth is named, that he would grant you, according to the riches of his glory, to be strengthened with might by his Spirit in the inner man; that Christ may dwell in your hearts by faith; that ye, being rooted and grounded in love, may be able to comprehend with all saints what is the breadth, and length, and depth, and height; and to know the love of Christ, which passeth knowledge, that ye might be filled with all the fulness of God."

Ask God to lead you to verses of Scripture that He desires to bring to pass in your spouse's life and then pray those passages. If your spouse is unsaved, have two people agree in prayer with you over an anointed cloth, then place the cloth under the mattress. When you are alone, kneel and pray God's Word by his/her bedside. God's powerful Word will work as your spouse sleeps. When you pray for any lost soul, you are praying the will of God because it is not His will "that any should perish, but that all should come to repentance" (II Peter 3:9).

In your prayer journal, leave spaces for dated answers to every prayer. It is faith-building to look back and see God's marvelous answers. The best gift you can give to your spouse is to pray the Word in faith over his/her life.

In faith, pray the following verses of Scripture for your spouse:

I Chronicles 4:10
"Oh that thou wouldest bless me indeed, and enlarge my coast, and that thine hand might be with me, and that thou wouldest keep me from evil, that it may not grieve me!"

I Chronicles 17:27
"Let it please thee to bless the house of thy servant, that it may be before thee for ever: for thou blessest, O Lord, and it shall be blessed for ever."

Job 22:18
"He filled their houses with good things."

Malachi 2:6
"The law of truth was in his mouth, and iniquity was not found in his lips: he walked with me in peace and equity."

Philippians 1:6

"Being confident of this very thing, that he which hath begun a good work in you will perform it until the day of Jesus Christ."

Colossians 1:9-11

"For this cause we also, since the day we heard it, do not cease to pray for you, and to desire that ye might be filled with the knowledge of his will in all wisdom and spiritual understanding; that ye might walk worthy of the Lord unto all pleasing, being fruitful in every good work, and increasing in the knowledge of God; strengthened with all might, according to his glorious power, unto all patience and longsuffering with joyfulness."

Following the Will of God

Learn to pray the following concepts of the Word into your own situation. Study carefully and ask God to give you grace to obey His Word in all your circumstances.

● Leadership/Conviction for the Household

Joshua 24:15

> "And if it seem evil unto you to serve the LORD, choose you this day whom ye will serve; whether the gods which your fathers served that were on the other side of the flood, or the gods of the Amorites, in whose land ye dwell: but as for me and my house, we will serve the LORD."

Pray this verse of Scripture the following way:

Lord, help me to make a conscious decision every day to serve You—that I would not serve the gods of the world or continue traditions that have been passed down through my family, but that I could along with my entire household serve You with a sincere heart.

● Faithful Leader of the Home

I Timothy 3:4-5

> "One that ruleth well his own house, having his children in subjection with all gravity; (for if a man know not how to rule his own house, how shall he take care of the church of God?)."

● Founded in the Word

II Timothy 3:14-15

> "But continue thou in the things which thou hast learned and hast been assured of, knowing of whom thou hast learned them; and that from a child thou hast known the holy scriptures, which are able to make thee wise unto salvation through faith which is in Christ Jesus."

Titus 1:9

> "Holding fast the faithful word as he hath been taught, that he may be able by sound doctrine both to exhort and to convince the gainsayers."

● Making Good Decisions for the Home

Lot's bad choice

Genesis 13:10-11

> "And Lot lifted up his eyes, and beheld all the plain of Jordan, that it was well watered every where, before the LORD destroyed Sodom and Gomorrah, even as the garden of the LORD, like the land of Egypt, as thou comest unto Zoar. Then Lot chose him all the plain of Jordan; and Lot journeyed east: and they separated themselves the one from the other."

Versus Abraham's good choice

Genesis 18:19
> "For I know him, that he will command his children and his household after him, and they shall keep the way of the LORD, to do justice and judgment; that the LORD may bring upon Abraham that which he hath spoken of him."

● Follow God's Order for the Home

Ephesians 5:22-26, 28
> "Wives, submit yourselves unto your own husbands, as unto the Lord. For the husband is the head of the wife, even as Christ is the head of the church: and he is the saviour of the body. Therefore as the church is subject unto Christ, so let the wives be to their own husbands in every thing. Husbands, love your wives, even as Christ also loved the church, and gave himself for it; that he might sanctify and cleanse it with the washing of water by the word ... So ought men to love their wives as their own bodies. He that loveth his wife loveth himself."

● Wisdom with Resultant Benefits

Proverbs 3:13-14
> "Happy is the man that findeth wisdom, and the man that getteth understanding. For the merchandise of it is better than the merchandise of silver, and the gain thereof than fine gold."

Proverbs 3:21-24
> "My son, let not them depart from thine eyes: keep sound wisdom and discretion: so shall they be life unto thy soul,

and grace to thy neck. Then shalt thou walk in thy way safely, and thy foot shall not stumble. When thou liest down, thou shalt not be afraid: yea, thou shalt lie down, and thy sleep shall be sweet."

● Walk in the Ways of God

Psalm 25:4-5

"Shew me thy ways, O LORD; teach me thy paths. Lead me in thy truth, and teach me: for thou art the God of my salvation; on thee do I wait all the day."

Psalm 25:12

"What man is he that feareth the LORD? him shall he teach in the way that he shall choose."

Financial Blessings

Deuteronomy 8:18

"But thou shalt remember the Lord thy God: for it is he that giveth thee power to get wealth, that he may establish his covenant which he sware unto thy fathers, as it is to this day."

Pray the following prayer for any member of your family, being sure to read the Scripture text before and after the above passage:

Dear Father, I thank You for the knowledge You have given me in meeting the needs of life. Help me never to forget that it is You that gives me health and strength and the power to work and provide for my financial welfare. You gave me that power, Lord. Help me to use it wisely and to claim, through a holy lifestyle, the covenants You established and the promises You made to those who would walk upright before You. Thank You for helping me to understand that the work of Your kingdom must be first in my life, and that as I give, You will in turn give back to me; that You will provide my needs according to Your riches in glory so long as I obey Your precepts and remember that it is in You that I live and move and have my being.

Deuteronomy 7:12-13

"Wherefore it shall come to pass, if ye hearken to these judgments, and keep, and do them, that the LORD thy God shall keep unto thee the covenant and the mercy which he sware unto thy fathers: and he will love thee, and bless thee, and multiply thee: he will also bless the fruit of thy womb, and the fruit of thy land, thy corn, and thy wine, and thine oil, the increase of thy kine, and the flocks of thy sheep, in the land which he sware unto thy fathers to give thee."

Psalm 68:19

"Blessed be the Lord, who daily loadeth us with benefits, even the God of our salvation. Selah."

Psalm 112:1-9

"Praise ye the LORD. Blessed is the man that feareth the LORD, that delighteth greatly in his commandments. His seed shall be mighty upon earth: the generation of the upright shall be blessed. Wealth and riches shall be in his house: and his righteousness endureth for ever. Unto the upright there ariseth light in the darkness: he is gracious, and full of compassion, and righteous. A good man sheweth favour, and lendeth: he will guide his affairs with discretion. Surely he shall not be moved for ever: the righteous shall be in everlasting remembrance. He shall not be afraid of evil tidings: his heart is fixed, trusting in the LORD. His heart is established, he shall not be afraid, until he see his desire upon his enemies. He hath dispersed, he hath given to the poor; his righteousness endureth for ever; his horn shall be exalted with honour."

Proverbs 3:9-10

"Honour the LORD with thy substance, and with the firstfruits of all thine increase: so shall thy barns be filled with plenty, and thy presses shall burst out with new wine."

Proverbs 10:22

"The blessing of the Lord, it maketh rich, and he addeth no sorrow with it."

Isaiah 48:17

"Thus saith the Lord, thy Redeemer, the Holy One of Israel; I am the Lord thy God which teacheth thee to profit, which leadeth thee by the way that thou shouldest go."

Malachi 3:10-11

"Bring ye all the tithes into the storehouse, that there may be meat in mine house, and prove me now herewith, saith the Lord of hosts, if I will not open you the windows of heaven, and pour you out a blessing, that there shall not be room enough to receive it. And I will rebuke the devourer for your sakes, and he shall not destroy the fruits of your ground; neither shall your vine cast her fruit before the time in the field, saith the Lord of hosts."

Luke 6:38

"Give, and it shall be given unto you; good measure, pressed down, and shaken together, and running over, shall men give into your bosom. For with the same measure that ye mete withal it shall be measured to you again."

II Corinthians 9:7-8

"Every man according as he purposeth in his heart, so let him give; not grudgingly, or of necessity: for God loveth a cheerful giver. And God is able to make all grace abound toward you; that ye, always having all sufficiency in all things, may abound to every good work."

Prayer for Protection

Isaiah 43:2

"When thou passest through the waters, I will be with thee; and through the rivers, they shall not overflow thee: when thou walkest through the fire, thou shalt not be burned; neither shall the flame kindle upon thee."

Pray this:

Lord, no matter my circumstance, no matter the trials that I go through, help me to understand that Your Word has great and precious promises, and that You are faithful and will fulfill Your Word. Let me realize there is nothing that comes against me that will be greater than the power of Your Spirit that guides and keeps me. Help me to study the lives of those in Your Word that suffered and yet were not dismayed, to understand that You are the Master of all situations and will uphold me so that I will not lose my trust and faith in You.

Pray and search out these and other verses of Scripture for whatever is happening in your life. Use them for a shield from the experiences you will face.

Deuteronomy 31:8

"And the LORD, he it is that doth go before thee; he will be with thee, he will not fail thee, neither forsake thee: fear not, neither be dismayed."

Deuteronomy 33:27

"The eternal God is thy refuge, and underneath are the everlasting arms: and he shall thrust out the enemy from before thee; and shall say, Destroy them."

I Chronicles 4:10

"And Jabez called on the God of Israel, saying, Oh that thou wouldest bless me indeed, and enlarge my coast, and that thine hand might be with me, and that thou wouldest keep me from evil, that it may not grieve me! And God granted him that which he requested."

Joshua 1:9

"Have not I commanded thee? Be strong and of a good courage; be not afraid, neither be thou dismayed: for the LORD thy God is with thee whithersoever thou goest."

Psalm 35:4

"Let them be confounded and put to shame that seek after my soul: let them be turned back and brought to confusion that devise my hurt."

Psalm 121:8

"The LORD shall preserve thy going out and thy coming in from this time forth, and even for evermore."

Isaiah 41:10

"Fear thou not; for I am with thee: be not dismayed; for I am thy God: I will strengthen thee; yea, I will help thee; yea, I will uphold thee with the right hand of my righteousness."

Isaiah 54:17

"No weapon that is formed against thee shall prosper; and every tongue that shall rise against thee in judgment thou shalt condemn. This is the heritage of the servants of the LORD, and their righteousness is of me, saith the LORD."

II Thessalonians 3:3

"But the Lord is faithful, who shall stablish you, and keep you from evil."

Prayers for
the Workplace

One of the most challenging areas of our lives can be the workplace. At one point or another, almost everyone will face an awkward situation on the job. Our ethics and honesty may be tested or our faith questioned. It may be a difficult coworker or an unreasonable boss. Whatever the situation, it is important that we maintain our integrity and do nothing that would mar our Christian witness.

The Bible offers us many guidelines that will help us in the workplace. Consider the following passages, and ask God to help you in your dealings with others according to His Word.

⬤ Integrity and a Good Christian Witness

Proverbs 11:3
> "The integrity of the upright shall guide them."

Proverbs 16:32
> "He that is slow to anger is better than the mighty; and he that ruleth his spirit than he that taketh a city."

Luke 6:36-37
> "Be ye therefore merciful, as your Father also is merciful. Judge not, and ye shall not be judged: condemn not, and ye shall not be condemned: forgive, and ye shall be forgiven."

Luke 6:38

"Give, and it shall be given unto you; good measure, pressed down, and shaken together, and running over, shall men give into your bosom. For with the same measure that ye mete withal it shall be measured to you again."

I Peter 2:12

"Having your conversation honest among the Gentiles: that, whereas they speak against you as evildoers, they may by your good works, which they shall behold, glorify God in the day of visitation."

I Peter 3:13-16

"And who is he that will harm you, if ye be followers of that which is good? But and if ye suffer for righteousness' sake, happy are ye: and be not afraid of their terror, neither be troubled; but sanctify the Lord God in your hearts: and be ready always to give an answer to every man that asketh you a reason of the hope that is in you with meekness and fear: having a good conscience; that, whereas they speak evil of you, as of evildoers, they may be ashamed that falsely accuse your good conversation in Christ."

● Relationships on the Job

I Samuel 18:5

"And David went out whithersoever Saul sent him, and behaved himself wisely: and Saul set him over the men of war, and he was accepted in the sight of all the people, and also in the sight of Saul's servants."

Luke 6:31

"And as ye would that men should do to you, do ye also to them likewise."

John 13:34-35

"A new commandment I give unto you, That ye love one another; as I have loved you, that ye also love one another. By this shall all men know that ye are my disciples, if ye have love one to another."

Romans 13:7-8

"Render therefore to all their dues: tribute to whom tribute is due; custom to whom custom; fear to whom fear; honour to whom honour. Owe no man any thing, but to love one another: for he that loveth another hath fulfilled the law."

Colossians 3:12-14

"Put on therefore, as the elect of God, holy and beloved, bowels of mercies, kindness, humbleness of mind, meekness, longsuffering; forbearing one another, and forgiving one another, if any man have a quarrel against any: even as Christ forgave you, so also do ye. And above all these things put on charity, which is the bond of perfectness."

Colossians 4:1

"Masters, give unto your servants that which is just and equal; knowing that ye also have a Master in heaven."

⬤ Favor with Supervisory People

Ephesians 6:5-8

"Servants, be obedient to them that are your masters according to the flesh, with fear and trembling, in singleness of your heart, as unto Christ; not with eyeservice, as menpleasers; but as the servants of Christ, doing the will of God from the heart; with good will doing service, as to the Lord, and not to men: knowing that whatsoever good thing any man doeth, the same shall he receive of the Lord, whether he be bond or free."

Pray for your employer or supervisor:

Dear Lord, help me to be obedient to the people I work for so long as I can still follow You. Help me to realize that they are just flesh, the same as I am. Help me to realize that when I please them with my work that I am also fulfilling Your Word and doing it as unto You. May I learn obedience in any area that I may draw closer to You. Help me to see and understand that when I do any good thing for others that I will receive the same from You. Lord, I know that this will make it easier for me to do what seems to be difficult if I realize that You are the One who watches over me and sees all my actions and, just as importantly, my attitudes.

Proverbs 3:3-6

"Let not mercy and truth forsake thee: bind them about thy neck; write them upon the table of thine heart: so shalt thou find favour and good understanding in the sight of God and man. Trust in the Lord with all thine heart; and lean not unto thine own understanding. In all thy ways acknowledge him, and he shall direct thy paths."

Proverbs 3:35

"The wise shall inherit glory: but shame shall be the promotion of fools."

Proverbs 4:7-9

"Wisdom is the principal thing; therefore get wisdom: and with all thy getting get understanding. Exalt her, and she shall promote thee: she shall bring thee to honour, when thou dost embrace her. She shall give to thine head an ornament of grace: a crown of glory shall she deliver to thee."

Proverbs 12:8
"A man shall be commended according to his wisdom: but he that is of a perverse heart shall be despised."

Proverbs 12:24
"The hand of the diligent shall bear rule: but the slothful shall be under tribute."

Proverbs 14:19
"The evil bow before the good; and the wicked at the gates of the righteous."

Proverbs 17:2
"A wise servant shall have rule over a son that causeth shame, and shall have part of the inheritance among the brethren."

Proverbs 22:4
"By humility and the fear of the LORD are riches, and honour, and life."

Proverbs 22:11
"He that loveth pureness of heart, for the grace of his lips the king shall be his friend."

Proverbs 22:29
"Seest thou a man diligent in his business? he shall stand before kings; he shall not stand before mean men."

Jesus, help my eyes to see
All the good Thou sendest me.

Jesus, help my eyes to bear
Calls for help from far and near.

Jesus, help my feet to go
In the way that Thou wilt show.

Jesus, help my hands to do
All things loving, kind, and true.

Jesus, may I helpful be,
Growing every day like Thee.
Amen

(Author unknown)

Cleansing the Home

Psalm 101 was written when David brought the Ark of God back to Jerusalem. It had been gone for almost a century. David wanted the glory of God to return to Israel and realized preparation had to be made for this important event. He was willing to do whatever was necessary for the presence and glory of God to inhabit the House of Israel.

Psalm 101 is a clear pattern for us to cleanse our own home so the presence of God can dwell there and provide protection.

Read the entire psalm and then pray the verses as follows, or in your own words.

Psalm 101:1

Lord, I want to sing of Your goodness, kindness, and grace to my family and declare Your authority in my home.

Verse 2

Help us to act in wisdom, be faultless, upright, and honest in our way of life so that Your presence will fill our home. Let our home be a dwelling place where You are exalted so that our hearts will serve only You.

Verse 3

Please give us understanding and strength to remove from our home things that display or declare the wickedness of this world. Help my family to hate the things that might cause us to turn away from truth.

Verses 4-5, 7

Help us guard our home against any spirit of lying, pride, deceit, or immorality so that no way of life contrary to Your laws can enter.

Verse 6

Help us to look toward those who stand firm on Your Word as examples and as those we would welcome to minister to us in our home.

Verse 8

Give us Your power to help us withdraw from the morally wrong and to keep distress and sorrow from our home. Help our home to be a refuge for our family against the wickedness of the world.

Moral Purity

I Corinthians 10:13

> "There hath no temptation taken you but such as is common to man: but God is faithful, who will not suffer you to be tempted above that ye are able; but will with the temptation also make a way to escape, that ye may be able to bear it."

It is important no matter what our age to pray these verses of Scripture on morality. We must not ignore or fail to read and apply the Word of God to our life daily as follows:

Dear God, help me to remember that the same temptations have plagued man since the fall in the Garden of Eden. Keep me from thinking that there is something new in the world today that we have never faced before. Lord, if I should slip, help me to come to You immediately and not continue in my error. I do believe that You will not allow me to be tempted above that which I am able to overcome. Let Your Word and Your Spirit dwell in me richly and fully that I may glorify You with my life and my choices.

Job 31:1

> "I made a covenant with mine eyes; why then should I think upon a maid?"

Matthew 5:28

"But I say unto you, That whosoever looketh on a woman to lust after her hath committed adultery with her already in his heart."

Mark 7:21-23

"For from within, out of the heart of men, proceed evil thoughts, adulteries, fornications, murders, thefts, covetousness, wickedness, deceit, lasciviousness, an evil eye, blasphemy, pride, foolishness: all these evil things come from within, and defile the man."

Acts 15:29

"That ye abstain from meats offered to idols, and from blood, and from things strangled, and from fornication: from which if ye keep yourselves, ye shall do well. Fare ye well."

Galatians 5:16

"This I say then, Walk in the Spirit, and ye shall not fulfil the lust of the flesh."

Galatians 5:19

"Now the works of the flesh are manifest, which are these; Adultery, fornication, uncleanness, lasciviousness."

Ephesians 5:3

"But fornication, and all uncleanness, or covetousness, let it not be once named among you, as becometh saints."

Colossians 3:5-6

"Mortify therefore your members which are upon the earth; fornication, uncleanness, inordinate affection, evil concupiscence, and covetousness, which is idolatry: for which things' sake the wrath of God cometh on the children of disobedience."

I Thessalonians 4:3-5, 7

"For this is the will of God, even your sanctification, that ye should abstain from fornication: that every one of you should know how to possess his vessel in sanctification and honour; not in the lust of concupiscence, even as the Gentiles which know not God ... For God hath not called us unto uncleanness, but unto holiness."

Hebrews 12:16

"Lest there be any fornicator, or profane person, as Esau, who for one morsel of meat sold his birthright."

Hebrews 13:4

"Marriage is honourable in all, and the bed undefiled: but whoremongers and adulterers God will judge."

Revelation 21:8

"But the fearful, and unbelieving, and the abominable, and murderers, and whoremongers, and sorcerers, and idolaters, and all liars, shall have their part in the lake which burneth with fire and brimstone: which is the second death."

Spiritual
Discernment

Proverbs 2:9-11

"Then shalt thou understand righteousness, and judgment, and equity; yea, every good path. When wisdom entereth into thine heart, and knowledge is pleasant unto thy soul; discretion shall preserve thee, understanding shall keep thee."

Pray this for you and/or your spouse:

Lord, show [me/my spouse] Your ways and help us to seek Your direction in our home. Please guide us in the discernment of right and wrong for not only our lives, but the lives of each member of our family. When the enemy attempts to keep us from the paths of truth, please allow us clear judgment to follow after You.

I Kings 3:9

"Give therefore thy servant an understanding heart to judge thy people, that I may discern between good and bad: for who is able to judge this thy so great a people?"

Ecclesiastes 8:5

"Whoso keepeth the commandment shall feel no evil thing: and a wise man's heart discerneth both time and judgment."

Ezekiel 44:23

"And they shall teach my people the difference between the holy and profane, and cause them to discern between the unclean and the clean."

Malachi 3:18

"Then shall ye return, and discern between the righteous and the wicked, between him that serveth God and him that serveth him not."

I Corinthians 2:5-7

"That your faith should not stand in the wisdom of men, but in the power of God. Howbeit we speak wisdom among them that are perfect: yet not the wisdom of this world, nor of the princes of this world, that come to nought: but we speak the wisdom of God in a mystery, even the hidden wisdom, which God ordained before the world unto our glory."

I Corinthians 2:14

"But the natural man receiveth not the things of the Spirit of God: for they are foolishness unto him: neither can he know them, because they are spiritually discerned."

Ephesians 1:18

"The eyes of your understanding being enlightened; that ye may know what is the hope of his calling, and what the riches of the glory of his inheritance in the saints."

I Thessalonians 5:21

"Prove all things; hold fast that which is good."

I Timothy 4:7

"But refuse profane and old wives' fables, and exercise thyself rather unto godliness."

Hebrews 5:14

"But strong meat belongeth to them that are of full age, even those who by reason of use have their senses exercised to discern both good and evil."

Pray these verses in the same manner:

Psalm 37:23
Psalm 119:115
Proverbs 1:5
Proverbs 12:15
Philippians 1:9
Philippians 3:15

Praying for Prodigals
and the Lost

● Praying for Prodigals

Read the story of the prodigal son found in Luke 15:11-32.

While difficult times often precipitate people walking away from God, it is not the only reason they leave. Losing or never establishing a strong desire for the things of God is dangerous, and the enticement of this world is a continual draw. Regardless of what instigates a person's departure, the loss of even one individual from the body of Christ is devastating. The story of the prodigal son helps us understand all that is lost when someone walks away from God.

The prodigal son apparently felt he could handle his life better without his father's assistance. He demanded his share of his father's wealth and departed. After squandering all he had, his quality of life deteriorated. Thankfully, he came to himself and returned to his father's house. The father lovingly welcomed him, and their relationship was restored.

As you pray for one who has turned away from God, remind the Lord that the prodigal is one of His children. Pray that God will grant a space of repentance and that the prodigal would be able to receive His love and forgiveness. Some may have lived very sinful and immoral lives and cannot imagine the Father wanting them back.

Pray for love that would be open and warm to the prodigal while they are still in sin and not from a position of judgment or anger.

87

Extending love does not mean condoning their actions. Ask God for grace and persistence as it can take time to see the fruit of intercession.

Pray that whatever the prodigal is placing their trust in, outside of Jesus, would dry up. Pray that the novelty will wear off towards the things that hold them captive and for them to remember what it felt like to be in fellowship with God.

Pray and claim the following:

Isaiah 43:5-7
> "Fear not: for I am with thee: I will bring thy seed from the east, and gather thee from the west; I will say to the north, Give up; and to the south, Keep not back: bring my sons from far, and my daughters from the ends of the earth; even every one that is called by my name: for I have created him for my glory, I have formed him; yea, I have made him."

Using the above verses as a model, pray this awesome promise for your prodigal child:

Thank You, Lord, for the promise of Your Word. I claim that promise for my prodigal. I know it doesn't matter to You how far he has drifted because You covered the four corners of the earth in the promise to Isaiah concerning Your children. I realize this was promised concerning the seed of Abraham, but through Your shed blood, we have become children of the promise!

My prodigal has known Your grace, Lord, and was covered by Your blood in baptism, and in so doing took on Your name. According to Your Word, Lord, wherever he is now, north, south, east, or west, honor Your Word and speak to his heart. In Your mercy, grant him space for repentance. Stir him with a desire to surrender his life to You. He is not giving You glory in his present condition, but help him to pray as King David did, and create in him a clean heart and renew a right spirit within him. Just as You formed him, reform him now, I ask in Your name!

Pray this special prayer for the prodigal spouse:

Ephesians 1:17-19

"That the God of our Lord Jesus Christ, the Father of glory, may give unto you the spirit of wisdom and revelation in the knowledge of him: the eyes of your understanding being enlightened; that ye may know what is the hope of his calling, and what the riches of the glory of his inheritance in the saints, and what is the exceeding greatness of his power to us-ward who believe, according to the working of his mighty power."

Personalize the preceding Scripture verses the following way:

Oh, Heavenly Father, give my backslidden spouse the spirit of wisdom and revelation. Open his eyes to see what is right, and what the hope of his calling can be. Help him to see the riches of the glory of the inheritance that You have promised. Give her a vision of eternal punishment so that she will avoid that awful pit while at the same time seeing the wonderful exceeding greatness of Your power to transform and keep those who are believers of Your Word. I ask it in Your name and for Your glory. Amen.

As you pray the Word, turn these verses of Scripture into promises, and claim them for the glory of God.

Mark 11:24

"Therefore I say unto you, What things soever ye desire, when ye pray, believe that ye receive them, and ye shall have them."

Acts 2:39

"For the promise is unto you, and to your children, and to all that are afar off, even as many as the Lord our God shall call."

Acts 26:18

"To open their eyes, and to turn them from darkness to light, and from the power of Satan unto God, that they may receive forgiveness of sins, and inheritance among them which are sanctified by faith that is in me."

II Corinthians 4:4

"In whom the god of this world hath blinded the minds of them which believe not, lest the light of the glorious gospel of Christ, who is the image of God, should shine unto them."

II Peter 3:9

"The Lord is not slack concerning his promise, as some men count slackness; but is longsuffering to us-ward, not willing that any should perish, but that all should come to repentance."

Additional verses that you can pray:

Psalm 55:17
Psalm 103:12
Psalm 103:17
Psalm 138:3
Proverbs 20:7
Isaiah 44:22
Matthew 7:7-8
John 14:13-14
James 1:6
I John 1:9

● Pray for the attitude of the elder son.

The church (the elder brother) will need the Lord to prepare their hearts to receive the prodigals back. Pray that judgmental attitudes toward them would be gone. Pray against jealousy and envy as God's blessings pour on the prodigal and that they would lead many to the Lord. God does not show partiality. If blessings come to the prodigal, it will come to the other children too!

Hebrews 12:15
"Looking diligently lest any man fail of the grace of God; lest any root of bitterness springing up trouble you, and thereby many be defiled."

Psalm 86:5
"For thou, Lord, art good, and ready to forgive; and plenteous in mercy unto all them that call upon thee."

Matthew 6:14-15
"For if ye forgive men their trespasses, your heavenly Father will also forgive you: but if ye forgive not men their trespasses, neither will your Father forgive your trespasses."

Luke 6:37

"Judge not, and ye shall not be judged: condemn not, and ye shall not be condemned: forgive, and ye shall be forgiven."

II Corinthians 2:10-11

"To whom ye forgive any thing, I forgive also: for if I forgave any thing, to whom I forgave it, for your sakes forgave I it in the person of Christ; lest Satan should get an advantage of us: for we are not ignorant of his devices."

Malachi 3:16-17

"Then they that feared the Lord spake often one to another: and the Lord hearkened, and heard it, and a book of remembrance was written before him for them that feared the Lord, and that thought upon his name. And they shall be mine, saith the Lord of hosts, in that day when I make up my jewels; and I will spare them, as a man spareth his own son that serveth him."

⬤ Praying for the Lost

Perhaps your loved one has never known the Lord. You have prayed and prayed, but seemingly there are no results. Remember, it is God's desire for everyone to be saved, and this includes the one for whom you are fervently interceding. We must understand that "the god of this world hath blinded the minds of them which believe not" (II Corinthians 4:4).

I Timothy 2:4

"Who will have all men to be saved, and to come unto the knowledge of the truth."

Pray that God will change the heart of the person for whom you are praying, and that He will put a desire in his or her heart to serve Him.

Ezekiel 36:26-27

"A new heart also will I give you, and a new spirit will I put within you: and I will take away the stony heart out of your flesh, and I will give you an heart of flesh. And I will put my spirit within you, and cause you to walk in my statutes, and ye shall keep my judgments, and do them."

Lord, I pray that You will give [name] a new heart and put within [him/her] a new spirit. Take away their stony heart of sin and place within them a heart that is soft and tender toward You. Put Your Spirit within [name] so that [he/she] can walk in a way that is pleasing to You and obey Your laws and do them.

Ephesians 1:18

"The eyes of your understanding being enlightened; that ye may know what is the hope of his calling, and what the riches of the glory of his inheritance in the saints."

Isaiah 55:11

"So shall my word be that goeth forth out of my mouth: it shall not return unto me void, but it shall accomplish that which I please, and it shall prosper in the thing whereto I sent it."

Pray that the Lord will send other Spirit-filled believers into the life of your loved one who will be a positive influence and share God's truth with them.

Luke 10:2b

"Pray ye therefore the Lord of the harvest, that he would send forth labourers into his harvest."

Don't forget to pray that your life will be a witness as well. Pray that you will have the "mind of Christ" so that your words and actions will reflect the Lord that you serve.

Philippians 2:5
> "Let this mind be in you, which was also in Christ Jesus."

Additional verses that you can pray:

Jeremiah 24:7
Jeremiah 29:11-13
Luke 24:31, 45
Romans 10:17
II Corinthians 4:3-4
II Timothy 2:26
I Peter 3:1-5
I John 5:14-15

Prayer for
the Bible
Study Student

"Open thou mine eyes,
that I may behold wondrous
things out of thy law"
(Psalm 119:18).

"So shall my word be that goeth forth out of my mouth:
it shall not return unto me void,
but it shall accomplish that which I please,
and it shall prosper in the thing whereto I sent it"
(Isaiah 55:11).

Sowing
the Seed

We enter into an exciting endeavor when we begin to teach the Word of God to a hungry soul. Whether it is a longstanding friendship or a new acquaintance, there is no greater joy than sharing biblical truth and seeing that knowledge begin to grow in a heart. Yet, we also know that Satan likes nothing better than for the precious seed that we sow to remain lifeless, either never taking root or its tender shoots soon withering. It is vital that we do all we can to maintain the proper conditions for growth.

One of the most important steps we can take is to earnestly pray for the seed of the Word to take root and bring forth abundantly. Psalm 126:6 says, "He that goeth forth and weepeth, bearing precious seed, shall doubtless come again with rejoicing, bringing his sheaves with him." While prayer is not specifically mentioned, within this verse we sense the burden and concern of the sower. The farmer knows when he goes into the field that without the resulting harvest, there will be famine. All his efforts are devoted to allowing that seed to reproduce.

We, too, enter the fields with a sense of burden and responsibility. In the parable of the sower, Jesus said, "Then cometh the devil, and taketh away the word out of their hearts, lest they should believe and be saved" (Luke 8:12). We cannot allow this to happen. Satan's tactics can be defeated when our burden drives us to our knees. We can pray a defense around that soul so that the seed will take root and grow. "The effectual fervent prayer of a righteous man availeth much" (James 5:16).

Through prayer we will come rejoicing, bringing our sheaves with us.

- We must pray specifically for the person we are teaching that the Word of God would fall on a tender heart. We must also pray for ourselves that we may be able to impart knowledge to them as we speak the Word, that they will receive understanding from God.

- We may also pray the verses of Scripture under "Hunger and Revelation" for ourselves and for the student.

Hunger and Revelation

The following verses of Scripture on understanding and hunger for God and His Word have been edited for you in learning to pray the Word more effectively.

● Truth

Psalm 25:4-5

"Shew me thy ways, O LORD; teach me thy paths. Lead me in thy truth, and teach me: for thou art the God of my salvation; on thee do I wait all the day."

Show (name of person) thy ways, O Lord; teach (him/her) thy paths. Lead (him/her) in thy truth, and teach (him/her): for thou art the God of (his/her) salvation.

John 8:32

"And ye shall know the truth, and the truth shall make you free."

Lord, I pray that (name of person) shall know the truth, and the truth shall make (name of person) free.

John 16:13

"Howbeit when he, the Spirit of truth, is come, he will guide you into all truth: for he shall not speak of himself; but whatsoever he shall hear, that shall he speak: and he will shew you things to come."

Lord, I pray that when He, the Spirit of truth, is come, He will guide (name of person) into all truth. Lord, I pray that (name of person) shall know the truth, and the truth shall make (name of person) free.

● Faith

Romans 10:17

"So then faith cometh by hearing, and hearing by the word of God."

Hebrews 11:6

"But without faith it is impossible to please him: for he that cometh to God must believe that he is, and that he is a rewarder of them that diligently seek him."

Lord, I pray that (name of person) would have faith to hear and understand the Word of God. I pray that (he/she) would believe in You and know that You reward those who seek You diligently.

● The Word

Matthew 13:23

"But he that received seed into the good ground is he that heareth the word, and understandeth it; which also beareth fruit, and bringeth forth, some an hundredfold, some sixty, some thirty."

I pray that (name of person) would be one that receives the seed of the Word into good ground, that she/he would hear and understand the Word, and also bear fruit.

James 1:21-25

"Wherefore lay apart all filthiness and superfluity of naughtiness, and receive with meekness the engrafted word, which is able to save your souls. But be ye doers of the word, and not hearers only, deceiving your own selves. For if any be a hearer of the word, and not a doer, he is like unto a man beholding his natural face in a glass: for he beholdeth himself, and goeth his way, and straightway forgetteth what manner of man he was. But whoso looketh into the perfect law of liberty, and continueth therein, he being not a forgetful hearer, but a doer of the work, this man shall be blessed in his deed."

I pray that (name of person) would lay apart all filthiness and evil in (his/her) life, and receive with meekness the implanted Word, which is able to save (his/her) soul. Let (name of person) be a doer of the Word, and not a hearer only, deceiving (himself/herself).

● Seeking after God

Isaiah 55:6

"Seek ye the Lᴏʀᴅ while he may be found, call ye upon him while he is near."

Lord, I pray that (name of person) would seek the Lord while He may be found, and call upon Him while He is near.

Acts 17:27

"That they should seek the Lord, if haply they might feel after him, and find him, though he be not far from every one of us."

Lord, I pray that (name of person) should seek the Lord, if haply they might feel after Him, and find Him, though He be not far from every one of us.

● Spiritual Understanding

Look up the following verses of Scripture and pray them as shown.

Ephesians 1:17-19

I pray that the God of our Lord Jesus Christ, the Father of glory, may give unto (name of person) the spirit of wisdom and revelation in the knowledge of Him: the eyes of (his/her) understanding being enlightened; that (he/she) may know what is the hope of His calling, and what is the riches of the glory of His inheritance in the saints, and what is the exceeding greatness of His power to us-ward who believe, according to the working of His mighty power.

Colossians 1:9-11

For this cause we also, since the day we heard it, do not cease to pray for (name of person), and to desire that (he/she) might be filled with the knowledge of His will in all wisdom and spiritual understanding; that (name of person) might walk worthy of the Lord unto all pleasing, being fruitful in every good work, and increasing in the knowledge of God; strengthened with all might, according to His glorious power, unto all patience and longsuffering with joyfulness.

● Repentance

Acts 3:19

Lord, I pray that (name of person) would repent therefore, and be converted, that (his/her) sins may be blotted out, when the times of refreshing shall come from the presence of the Lord.

II Corinthians 7:10

Lord, I pray that (name of person) would experience godly sorrow which would work repentance to salvation.

● Baptism

Romans 6:4

> *Lord, I pray that (name of person) would be buried with Him by baptism into death: that like as Christ was raised up from the dead by the glory of the Father, even so (he/she) also should walk in newness of life.*

● Holy Ghost

Acts 1:8

> *Lord, I pray that (name of person) shall receive power, after that the Holy Ghost is come upon (him/her).*

Acts 2:4

> *Lord, I pray that (name of person) will be filled with the Holy Ghost, and begin to speak with other tongues, as the Spirit gives (him/her) utterance.*

● Completion of Work

Philippians 1:6

Lord, I am confident of this very thing, that He which hath begun a good work in (name of person) will perform it until the day of Jesus Christ.

Praying the Word in Times of Trouble

———————●———————

"For in the time of trouble he shall hide me in his pavilion:
in the secret of his tabernacle shall he hide me;
he shall set me up upon a rock"
(Psalm 27:5).

"When thou passest through the waters, I will be with thee;
and through the rivers, they shall not overflow thee:
when thou walkest through the fire, thou shalt not be burned;
neither shall the flame kindle upon thee"
(Isaiah 43:2).

The Disabled or Special Needs Child

"And the King shall answer and say unto them,
Verily I say unto you, Inasmuch as ye have done it unto one
of the least of these my brethren, ye have done it unto me"
(Matthew 25:40).

The world as a whole looks down on those born with noticeable defects. Abortion and euthanasia is an endeavor to rid the population of those who are not the "norm." In the animal kingdom the mother will destroy a baby with a difficulty; however, we are not animals. We were made in the image of God and so were our children.

In the eyes of the world, special need individuals are a worthless and dependent population. Due to the rising cost of health care, abortion and euthanasia seem like logical answers. This attitude is inaccurate. All of those associated with special need individuals realize the contributions these people make in changing our heart and minds and the way we view life.

In the eyes of God, these are special children. We call our son our "forever child." He will never earn a degree from a college, but he will be with us forever. We will never have to suffer the "empty nest syndrome" unless God calls him home ahead of us.

Being a mother of a special needs child who is now an adult, I would say it is not easy, but God knows how to give grace even in a difficult situation.

109

Forgiveness

Because the child is different, it is only natural to mourn what the child may miss out on in life. In my son's situation, marriage is out of the question. He sometimes will say, "I might get married some day." I must check myself to not allow bitterness to creep in and become jealous of his childhood friends when their weddings take place. Knowing that he will never have a child to carry on the family name is difficult.

The blame game is not a new game used in these situations. In the Bible we read of a young man who was blind (John 9). The game started with Jesus' disciples wanting to know who was to blame, him or his parents, for his blindness. Jesus had to set them straight. Neither he nor his parents were to blame.

All children must learn about forgiveness even if they are disabled. They will have to use it like all of humanity. The special needs child has normal human feelings and must learn to forgive others.

Self-Esteem

Both the parent and the child will battle with low self-esteem many times. A wheelchair usually evokes sympathy, but a mentally challenged child who looks normal may say off-the-wall things and most people cannot tolerate that. As parents we must be advocates for them, but we must understand that most people don't really understand what is going on in our child. We must remember that God has placed this child in our hands, and we are a caretaker of him or her. We must not let others dictate how we feel about ourselves. Keep in mind that God is looking in on the scene, and He will work it out. Our confidence is in Him.

The world views the disabled child by the things he cannot do, but God sees His abilities within the disability. The special needs child will often compare themselves to the norm, but it is important to stress that we are all unique. He has created us for His purpose, not for what we think we should be. His Word tells us that it is unwise to compare ourselves with others, and we must guard against comparison.

David sent for Mephibosheth, who was a descendant of Saul. Of course, Mephibosheth was scared to death because he just knew he was going to be killed because of Saul's treatment of David. We know the end of the story. He was taken in by the king and sat at the king's table. The story is most unusual for a king to take a crippled person into his house. Isn't that like the Lord? We are all messed up in some way and yet God welcomes us to His house. We are permitted to stay and even eat at His table.

Coping

Treat the special needs child as normal as possible, always keeping in mind their capabilities. Those in wheelchairs cannot run with their feet in the park, but someone can push them fast and make them feel a part of the outing.

Jennifer, a friend in our church who uses a wheelchair because of cerebral palsy, needed her shoe tied. As I bent to tie it, the Lord seemingly spoke to me from Scripture: "If you've done it to the least of these you have done it unto me." Whoa! What a privilege it is to help those who struggle.

When our son is feeling down and battling depression, we have something we do which really works. Instead of counting to ten, we say "Jesus" ten times, counting with our fingers. Almost always before we are off of one hand, the spirit of depression lifts and he begins to praise the Lord. The name of Jesus is powerful in any situation we might find ourselves.

Consider the following verses of Scripture and claim them as your very own. Personalize and pray the promises that are in the verses.

Psalm 139:14-17

"I will praise thee; for I am fearfully and wonderfully made: marvellous are thy works; and that my soul knoweth right well. My substance was not hid from thee, when I was made in secret, and curiously wrought in the lowest parts of the earth. Thine eyes did see my substance, yet being unperfect; and in thy book all my members were written, which in continuance were fashioned, when as yet there was none of them. How precious also are thy thoughts unto me, O God! How great is the sum of them!"

Matthew 19:13-14

"Then were there brought unto him little children, that he should put his hands on them, and pray: and the disciples rebuked them. But Jesus said, Suffer little children, and forbid them not, to come unto me: for of such is the kingdom of heaven."

Matthew 18:3

"And he said, Verily I say unto you, Except ye be converted, and become as little children, ye shall not enter into the kingdom of heaven."

John 9:2-3

"And his disciples asked him, saying, Master, who did sin, this man, or his parents, that he was born blind? Jesus answered, Neither hath this man sinned, nor his parents: but that the works of God should be made manifest in him."

Matthew 25:40

"And the King shall answer and say unto them, Verily I say unto you, Inasmuch as ye have done it unto one of the least of these my brethren, ye have done it unto me."

Jeremiah 29:11-12

"For I know the thoughts that I think toward you, saith the LORD, thoughts of peace, and not of evil, to give you an expected end. Then shall ye call upon me, and ye shall go and pray unto me, and I will hearken unto you."

When Stress Overwhelms Us

"Come unto me, all ye that labour and are heavy laden, and I will give you rest. Take my yoke upon you, and learn of me; for I am meek and lowly in heart: and ye shall find rest unto your souls" (Matthew 11:28-29).

It is not possible to live without stress. Originally the term came from physics—the application of sufficient force to an object to distort it. So, stress is really a transaction that takes place between us and our environment. Outside factors interact with our belief system; our brain interprets what's happening and tells our body how to respond. The body gets put on "red alert," adrenalin flows, and the "fight or flight" response kicks in.

Most of us are not subject to physical danger very often, but whenever we are "threatened" by an expectation we don't think we can meet, our body reacts in the same way.

The statistics don't lie:
- Stress now contributes to 90 percent of all diseases.
- Half of all visits to doctors are stress related.
- "Anxiety reduction" is one of today's largest businesses.
- More will die from stress-related illness than from infection or old age.
- Those in ministry are especially susceptible to stress.

The Menninger Foundation reports five most common feelings:

- Overextension (too many commitments, few boundaries)
- Imprecise competence (flying by the seat of my pants)
- Inadequate resources (running on the leftovers)
- Groping for relevant faith (idealism vs. realism)
- Lack of accomplishment (can't measure the intangible)

When we add these to "normal" stresses, look out!

Some stress is normal—and necessary! There is a good stress ("eustress") and bad stress ("distress") in our lives, but prolonged or frequent stress of any type is detrimental. Medical experts are now saying that there is an "adrenalin addiction" that is similar to the state of physiological arousal derived from a dependency on alcohol or nicotine.

What's the number one stressor today? Relationships. Why? Because there is no such thing as a perfect one. Because we can't put them on a predictable schedule. Because we can't control what happens. Because they take inordinate amounts of time and effort. Because we can't always resolve things. Because when we compete with people, we alienate them. Because our own personality traits cause most of the tension we feel in relating to others.

More accurately, it is our *expectations* in relationships that cause stress—because we expect others to think, act, and react just like us. No one stresses about anything they do not care about. Some people care too little; others care too much. We need balance.

Let's further clarify the word "stress" by looking at the real culprit:

Stress
- Normal and necessary
- Physical depletion
- "Post-adrenaline depression"
- Not a spiritual attack

Burnout
- Result of mismanaged stress
- Emotional exhaustion ("compassion fatigue")
- Like stress, leads to feelings of (deeper) depression—reaction not usually to "collapse" but to "go numb"
- "Imbalanced living" provides a foothold for the devil

Dr. Richard Swenson in his book *Margin: Restoring Emotional, Physical, Financial, and Time Reserves to Overloaded Lives* defines "margin" as "the amount allowed beyond that which is needed" or "the space that exists between ourselves and our limits." If overload is the disease of the new millennium, margin is the cure. No margin for an extended period of time is called burnout.

We cannot obey any of the following commands if there is not "white space" in our life.

- "And whosoever shall compel thee to go a mile, go with him twain" (Matthew 5:41).

- "Bear ye one another's burdens, and so fulfil the law of Christ" (Galatians 6:2).

- "As we have therefore opportunity, let us do good unto all men, especially unto them who are of the household of faith" (Galatians 6:10).

Pray and claim the following:

Psalm 103:2-5
> "Bless the Lord, O my soul, and forget not all his benefits: who forgiveth all thine iniquities; who healeth all thy diseases; who redeemeth thy life from destruction; who crowneth thee with lovingkindness and tender mercies; who satisfieth thy mouth with good things; so that thy youth is renewed like the eagle's."

Isaiah 40:31
> "But they that wait upon the Lord shall renew their strength; they shall mount up with wings as eagles; they shall run, and not be weary; and they shall walk, and not faint."

Lamentation 3:25-26
> "The Lord is good unto them that wait for him, to the soul that seeketh him. It is good that a man should both hope and quietly wait for the salvation of the Lord."

Matthew 11:28-29
> "Come unto me, all ye that labour and are heavy laden, and I will give you rest. Take my yoke upon you, and learn of me; for I am meek and lowly in heart: and ye shall find rest unto your souls."

Romans 8:25-26
> "But if we hope for that we see not, then do we with patience wait for it. Likewise the Spirit also helpeth our infirmities: for we know not what we should pray for as we ought: but the Spirit itself maketh intercession for us with groanings which cannot be uttered."

II Corinthians 12:9
> "And he said unto me, My grace is sufficient for thee: for my strength is made perfect in weakness. Most gladly

therefore will I rather glory in my infirmities, that the power of Christ may rest upon me."

Additional verses that you can pray:

Psalm 25:4-5
Psalm 25:20-21
Psalm 27:14
Psalm 37:7
Psalm 51:10-12
Psalm 62:5-7
Isaiah 14:3
Isaiah 30:15
Jeremiah 6:16
Jeremiah 14:22
Hosea 12:6
Micah 7:7-8
II Corinthians 4:16
Ephesians 4:23

The Battlefield
of the Mind

The mind is a laboratory—discovering, calculating, and concluding. The mind is a vault—concealing and secretive, storing all sorts of things that can be retrieved on a moment's notice. The mind is also a wellspring, spilling out what's been stored there. In fact, character is born in our thought life. "As he thinketh in his heart, so is he" (Proverbs 23:7).

Shakespeare described Hamlet's mental state. Human frailty and unmet needs and expectations tossed him on waves of doubt and indecision. Fueled by bitterness, his storm increased. He flailed about, seeking something or someone stable he could depend on—but in all the wrong places. Frustrated and dismayed, he thought hope was lost. His mind turned to ending his despair and on into a whirling vortex. Hamlet's famous soliloquy, "To be, or not to be," reveals the battle raging in his mind.

Perhaps the best analogy is to liken the mind to a battlefield. Just as on a natural battlefield, little things matter in our thought life. Thoughts are the seed of the deed. The enemy knows this—and that the flesh cooperates willingly in its own downfall.

Depression and defeat are favored tools of the enemy. Melancholy, introverted people may seem like natural targets for attacks of depression, but depression is no respecter of personality type. Thoughts that focus on the enemy's "mind-fields" place one squarely into the enemy's crosshairs and invite a spiritual attack.

While depression and morbid thoughts caused by chemical imbalances can be treated medically with success, no amount of Prozac can defeat a spiritual attack. In fact, for some, anti-depressants cause further depression and worse. Tranquilizers may mask symptoms, but they provide no real protection.

What Are the "Mind-fields"?

So what are the enemy's "mind-fields"? What thought patterns are most at risk?

- Bitterness
- Pride
- Condemnation
- Rebellion and stubbornness
- Envy and emulation
- Secret sins
- Fear, failure
- Unforgiveness
- Frustration and stress
- Unmet needs and expectations

Hidden within these "mind-fields" are the seeds of our soul's destruction. They cannot be masked and left to themselves, lest they sprout and bring forth a terrible harvest. In gardening, it does no good to chop off weeds at ground level. They just re-germinate and continue to plague good plants. Next year, the same weeds return, bringing lots of buddies. Superficial action is not enough. The only way to conquer them is to root them out.

Dear Jesus, "Let the words of my mouth, and the meditation of my heart, be acceptable in thy sight, O LORD, my strength, and my redeemer" (Psalm 19:14). I ask You to take authority over my thought life. Let my thoughts be according to Your Word. When they venture into the enemy's mind-fields, help me to gird up the loins of my mind and prove what is good and acceptable in Your sight. Help me to think on things that are true, honest, just, pure, lovely, of good report, of virtue, and praise (Philippians 4:8).

Where Is Our Refuge?

Of course it is in Jesus and His Word. When the enemy came tempting Him, Jesus responded with the Word, using it like a trowel. He spoke truth, cutting to the quick and exposing the root cause. As the Master Gardener, He waters good seed and fertilizes it with the promise of abundant and overcoming life. Yielded, willing obedience and seeking His help in seeing ourselves as He sees us are essential tools in the weeding and rebuilding process. Through reflecting upon His Word, He is able to transform our brokenness into His glorious image.

Dear Jesus, I bring to You a broken vessel. I've made a mess and cannot make it right. Even my thinking is flawed. I need total transformation from the inside out: thoughts, character, and mindset. Lead me in a plain path because the enemy of my soul is plotting my destruction. Help me to gain Your perspective and outlook. You are the potter; I am the clay. You do not just mend broken things—You heal them!

How do we pray against negative and destructive thoughts? Despair? Depression? Suicide? We pray for the mind of Christ. "Be renewed in the spirit of your mind" (Ephesians 4:23). We pray for the "quickening" of His Word (Psalm 119:154).

Pray these verses of Scripture:

Isaiah 26:3
> "Thou wilt keep him in perfect peace, whose mind is stayed on thee: because he trusteth in thee."

Micah 7:7-8

"Therefore I will look unto the Lord; I will wait for the God of my salvation: my God will hear me. Rejoice not against me, O mine enemy: when I fall, I shall arise; when I sit in darkness, the Lord shall be a light unto me."

Romans 12:1-2

"I beseech you therefore, brethren, by the mercies of God, that ye present your bodies a living sacrifice, holy, acceptable unto God, which is your reasonable service. And be not conformed to this world: but be ye transformed by the renewing of your mind, that ye may prove what is that good, and acceptable, and perfect, will of God."

II Corinthians 10:3-6

"For though we walk in the flesh, we do not war after the flesh: (for the weapons of our warfare are not carnal, but mighty through God to the pulling down of strong holds;) casting down imaginations, and every high thing that exalteth itself against the knowledge of God, and bringing into captivity every thought to the obedience of Christ; and having in a readiness to revenge all disobedience, when your obedience is fulfilled."

Philippians 2:5

"Let this mind be in you, which was also in Christ Jesus."

Additional verses that you can pray:

Psalm 27
Psalm 61
Psalm 86
Psalm 103:8-18
Psalm 107:19-21
John 17 (Jesus' prayer for you)
Galatians 5:22-23
Ephesians 6:11-18
I Timothy 4:12-16
II Timothy 1:5-7

Divorce and Children
of Divorce

In this journey of life, we are often faced with trials and circumstances we do not desire. However, they can bring us closer to our Lord and help us understand His great love for us.

If we were never brokenhearted, we would not know Him as our comforter, the God who heals the brokenhearted. If we had all we desired, we would not know Him as our provider. Through our trials we learn He is our deliverer, our source of hope, our protector, and our conqueror.

● The Necessity of Forgiveness

When divorce divides a home, we may feel it is impossible to forgive. Forgiveness does not absolve the ex-spouse of his or her responsibility. It releases us from being bitter. To walk in forgiveness is to walk in the power of God. God's Word says we must forgive others as He has forgiven us.

Staying captive to old hurts is a choice. Make the choice to no longer be victim to them. Experience the freedom of forgiveness! A lack of forgiveness is a bitter root of iniquity in our heart, which will defile those around us, especially our children. If we fail to model forgiveness for the children, they won't know how to forgive. Then they won't heal.

When your child desires to have a relationship or spend time with the ex-spouse, you may feel hurt. If you feel this way, please pray the forgiveness prayer below for yourself and your child. Don't force him to choose between his parents. She doesn't love you less because she loves the ex-spouse. Your child loves you both and needs you both to love him.

Pray:

Lord, change my heart and help me to forgive. Uproot any bitterness in my life. Let all bitterness, anger, wrath, clamor, and evil speaking be put away from me with all malice and strife. Help me to forgive completely, even as You have forgiven me. Help me to forget the past and look forward for both myself and my child.

Place a new dimension of love in my heart for my child. Let my actions overflow with motherly/fatherly affection for this precious child You have given me. Restore our relationship to reflect Your love and grace. Help my child to forgive me and my ex-spouse. Remove my fear of rejection by my child and help me to recognize his heart is big enough to love both me and the ex-spouse.

Pray the following after making it personal:

Ephesians 4:31-32
> "Let all bitterness, and wrath, and anger, and clamour, and evil speaking, be put away from you, with all malice: and be ye kind one to another, tenderhearted, forgiving one another, even as God for Christ's sake hath forgiven you."

Show them by your love and from the Word of God that they are very important to you and to God and that they can always depend on Him. Help them to take Scripture to heart and live with the sweet assurance of the words.

Psalm 139:13-18

"For thou hast possessed my reins: thou hast covered me in my mother's womb. I will praise thee; for I am fearfully and wonderfully made: marvellous are thy works; and that my soul knoweth right well. My substance was not hid from thee, when I was made in secret, and curiously wrought in the lowest parts of the earth. Thine eyes did see my substance, yet being unperfect; and in thy book all my members were written, which in continuance were fashioned, when as yet there was none of them. How precious also are thy thoughts unto me, O God! how great is the sum of them! If I should count them, they are more in number than the sand: when I awake, I am still with thee."

Isaiah 43:18

"Remember ye not the former things, neither consider the things of old."

Luke 6:37

"Judge not, and ye shall not be judged: condemn not, and ye shall not be condemned: forgive, and ye shall be forgiven."

Note: *Forgiveness does not mean leaving the child in a situation where they are emotionally or physically abused, neglected, or not protected. It is your duty as a parent to love and protect them.*

● Emotional Needs of the Child

Many homes have been devastated by divorce. As difficult as it is for the adults involved, the frequently overlooked victim is the child. Children of divorce literally feel torn within themselves. They often do not have a complete sense of self separate from their parents. To choose between the parents rips them apart emotionally. They long for their parents to be together and to feel safe, secure, and loved.

This is not a onetime event for the child. It is a daily hurt. It is imperative we cover the child in prayer so that we can rear emotionally healthy children, who in turn become emotionally whole adults and break the curse of divorce. The prayer of God's Word can heal and repair the breach.

Isaiah 55:11

"So shall my word be that goeth forth out of my mouth: it shall not return unto me void, but it shall accomplish that which I please, and it shall prosper in the thing whereto I sent it."

Pray:

Dear Lord, I come before You today, standing in the gap for my child, believing Your Word. You have said Your Word will not come back void, but it shall accomplish that which You please and it shall prosper in the thing which You sent it. I pray that Your Word shall go forth in righteousness. Protect and preserve this child and let Your Word dwell in him richly in all wisdom.

Read the following verses of Scripture with your child and then pray and claim the promises.

Psalm 27:10

"When my father and my mother forsake me, then the LORD will take me up."

Proverbs 30:5

"Every word of God is pure: he is a shield unto them that put their trust in him."

Isaiah 25:4

"For thou hast been a strength to the poor, a strength to the needy in his distress, a refuge from the storm, a shadow from the heat, when the blast of the terrible ones is as a storm against the wall."

Isaiah 40:29-31

"He giveth power to the faint; and to them that have no might he increaseth strength. Even the youths shall faint and be weary, and the young men shall utterly fall: but they that wait upon the LORD shall renew their strength; they shall mount up with wings as eagles; they shall run, and not be weary; and they shall walk, and not faint."

Lamentations 3:22-23

"It is of the LORD's mercies that we are not consumed, because his compassions fail not. They are new every morning: great is thy faithfulness."

Deuteronomy 32:10

"He found him in a desert land, and in the waste howling wilderness; he led him about, he instructed him, he kept him as the apple of his eye."

Pray:

I call on You, most faithful God, to be a strong tower in this storm my child is passing through. Give me wisdom concerning the pain my child is going through. Reveal Yourself to him, I pray, and help us both to learn to know You in Your mercy and forgiveness. Be our shelter and our song. Keep my child in these difficult times. Wrap Your loving arms around us both and be our comfort and guide as we begin anew.

● Self-Esteem

The self-esteem of our children is constantly being assaulted. The media and their peers tell them if they aren't wealthy, smart, cool, or beautiful, they aren't valuable. If that isn't hard enough, when one parent leaves, they feel rejected by the people they need most to be their immoveable foundation. God can take the shattered pieces of their lives and fill it with His joy and peace.

Isaiah 44:2a
"Thus saith the Lord that made thee, and formed thee from the womb, which will help thee; Fear not."

Jeremiah 1:5a
"Before I formed thee in the belly I knew thee; and before thou camest forth out of the womb I sanctified thee."

Matthew 18:10
"Take heed that ye despise not one of these little ones; for I say unto you, That in heaven their angels do always behold the face of my Father which is in heaven."

Jeremiah 29:11-12
"For I know the thoughts that I think toward you, saith the Lord, thoughts of peace, and not of evil, to give you an expected end. Then shall ye call upon me, and ye shall go and pray unto me, and I will hearken unto you."

Pray:

Lord, I pray You help me to realize how completely You love me and help me to reflect Your love to this child. Help us both to know You created and fashioned us in perfection, before we were ever born. You laid our lives out before us and knew every choice we would make. We are precious to You. Help us to have the right perspective on how You view us.

I pray this child will fully realize the depth of Your love and not be conformed to this world, but be conformed to the very image of You. Let this child be a pure vessel of honor, character, and integrity to be used by the Master's hand for His glory. Let their light reflect the love and joy of the Lord. Let them walk in the strength and knowledge that they are a peculiar people, a royal priesthood, a chosen generation, called into the marvelous light of the Lord. May they walk in holiness. Keep them as the apple of Your eye and guide their steps.

God, direct my day and my time so that I can spend the time with my child that he needs. Give me the energy and strength to relate with my child and help him to feel special. Help me to see and appreciate the unique qualities You have placed within him and help me to love him unconditionally.

● Healing

The prayers of a parent can pave the way for God to be real to his or her children. He can become their father or mother and fill the void in their lives.

The attention we lavish upon our children is a healing force in itself, but God can do a work and heal the hurts we cannot begin to understand. His word declares He bore our sorrows and our transgressions, and by the stripes He received, we are healed. He sent forth His Word and healed us. He gives beauty for ashes, the oil of joy for mourning, and the garment of praise for the spirit of heaviness!

Healing of Childhood Sexual Abuse

Sexual abuse, regardless of the number of times it occurred, the identity of the perpetrator, or the severity of the abuse inevitably causes the victim to feel helpless, confused, and rejected by God. This torrent of emotions is more than any child or adolescent can bear. A significant percentage of sexually abused children do not deal with their abuse until their adult years. Exposing the wound, facing the shame, and trusting someone enough to confess can take a very long time.

Happy marriages, healthy children, or successful careers have no power to erase the raw memories of the past. Regardless of how much she talks about it, how many self-help books she reads, or how much friends try to help, a mountain of hurt persists in her soul. This monolith of pain will simply not budge through any amount of human effort.

God can bring healing to the victim of sexual abuse. His Word is filled with countless promises which, when applied, will bring glorious victory and abundant life. His Word reshapes her thinking and brings light to the darkness in her heart caused by abuse.

The Path of Healing

The precious gift of spiritual rebirth required that Jesus suffer a humiliating death. If you are the victim of abuse, to partake in this gift and find freedom from your pain you also must be crucified with Christ. When you catch a vision of the cross, you will find there is no room in your heart or mind to dwell on the pain of the past. You will experience real deliverance and be able to freely love as you have been loved by God. This means you cannot blame the abuse for your bitterness and refusal to forgive. You cannot allow the past to hinder what God desires to accomplish in your life.

Exposing your wound to the Great Physician is your first step. Fear must give way to faith, sorrow to the joy of the Lord, and hatred must bow in the presence of God's agape love. Acknowledge that getting through this is not something you can do on your own.

Tell God you are willing to open the door of your heart to become "a new creation in Christ" (II Corinthians 5:17, NKJV). The ways of the world are not the ways of God. They may have wounded, confused, and disappointed us, but the painful events of life do not have to shape and define who we are.

The Word of God is precious and life-changing. What assurance He gives to those who will hear it and obey. Letting go of your past and the wrongs that have been committed against you is an act of worship to God.

Read the following verses of Scripture and then personalize them as you pray.

Isaiah 61:1

> "The Spirit of the Lord GOD is upon me; because the LORD hath anointed me to preach good tidings unto the meek; he hath sent me to bind up the brokenhearted, to proclaim liberty to the captives, and the opening of the prison to them that are bound."

Using the above verse as a model, pray this prayer for your situation:

Lord, You promised to heal the brokenhearted. My heart is broken. I am held captive by my thoughts of what has happened to me; I am bound as if in a prison. Release me from my captivity and make me free.

Psalm 6:2-3

"Have mercy on me, O Lord, for I am weak; O Lord, heal me, for my bones are troubled. My soul also is greatly troubled" (NKJV).

Psalm 18:6

"In my distress I called upon the Lord, and cried unto my God: he heard my voice out of his temple, and my cry came before him, even into his ears."

Psalm 51:10-11

"Create in me a clean heart, O God; and renew a right spirit within me. Cast me not away from thy presence; and take not thy holy spirit from me."

Romans 6:6

"Knowing this, that our old man is crucified with him, that the body of sin might be destroyed, that henceforth we should not serve sin."

Romans 12:2a

"And be not conformed to this world: but be ye transformed by the renewing of your mind."

Philippians 2:5

"Let this mind be in you, which was also in Christ Jesus."

Isaiah 43:18-19

"Remember ye not the former things, neither consider the things of old. Behold, I will do a new thing; now it shall spring forth; shall ye not know it? I will even make a way in the wilderness, and rivers in the desert."

Isaiah 61:3

"To give unto them beauty for ashes, the oil of joy for mourning, the garment of praise for the spirit of heaviness; that they might be called trees of righteousness."

Additional verses that you can pray:

Psalm 55:16-17
Psalm 119:28
Psalm 119:92
Psalm 119:133
Mark 11:25-26
Luke 6:28
Luke 23:34a
II Corinthians 5:17
II Corinthians 10:5
Philippians 4:13

Prayer for Healing

God has given many promises in His Word that confirm His desire to heal us. Whether our need is physical or emotional health, God has provided for our healing through the stripes that He bore on His body.

Claim the following verses of Scripture as you pray for healing.

● God Desires Us to be Healed

I Thessalonians 5:23

"And the very God of peace sanctify you wholly; and I pray God your whole spirit and soul and body be preserved blameless unto the coming of our Lord Jesus Christ."

James 5:14-15

"Is any sick among you? let him call for the elders of the church; and let them pray over him, anointing him with oil in the name of the Lord: and the prayer of faith shall save the sick, and the Lord shall raise him up; and if he have committed sins, they shall be forgiven him."

III John 2

"Beloved, I wish above all things that thou mayest prosper and be in health, even as thy soul prospereth."

● He Promises to Heal

Exodus 15:26

"If thou wilt diligently hearken to the voice of the Lord thy God, and wilt do that which is right in his sight, and wilt give ear to his commandments, and keep all his statutes, I will put none of these diseases upon thee, which I have brought upon the Egyptians: for I am the Lord that healeth thee."

Exodus 23:25

"Ye shall serve the Lord your God, and he shall bless thy bread, and thy water; and I will take sickness away from the midst of thee."

Psalm 103:1-3

"Bless the Lord, O my soul: and all that is within me, bless his holy name. Bless the Lord, O my soul, and forget not all his benefits: who forgiveth all thine iniquities; who healeth all thy diseases."

Isaiah 41:10

"Fear not, for I am with you; be not dismayed, for I am your God. I will strengthen you, Yes, I will help you, I will uphold you with My righteous right hand" (NKJV).

Malachi 4:2a

"But unto you that fear my name shall the Sun of righteousness arise with healing in his wings."

John 10:10

"The thief cometh not, but for to steal, and to kill, and to destroy: I am come that they might have life, and that they might have it more abundantly."

He Hears Our Prayers

Psalm 107:19-20

"Then they cry unto the LORD in their trouble, and he saveth them out of their distresses. He sent his word, and healed them, and delivered them from their destructions."

Mark 11:24

"Therefore I say unto you, What things soever ye desire, when ye pray, believe that ye receive them, and ye shall have them."

John 16:23b

"Verily, verily, I say unto you, Whatsoever ye shall ask the Father in my name, he will give it you."

I John 5:14-15

"And this is the confidence that we have in him, that, if we ask any thing according to his will, he heareth us: and if we know that he hear us, whatsoever we ask, we know that we have the petitions that we desired of him."

His Word Is Powerful to Heal

Psalm 107:20

"He sent his word, and healed them, and delivered them from their destructions."

Isaiah 55:11

"So shall my word be that goeth forth out of my mouth: it shall not return unto me void, but it shall accomplish that which I please, and it shall prosper in the thing whereto I sent it."

Jeremiah 1:12

"Then said the Lᴏʀᴅ unto me, Thou hast well seen: for I will hasten my word to perform it."

Matthew 8:16

"When the even was come, they brought unto him many that were possessed with devils: and he cast out the spirits with his word, and healed all that were sick."

● We Are Healed by His Stripes

Isaiah 53:5

"He was wounded for our transgressions, he was bruised for our iniquities: the chastisement of our peace was upon him; and with his stripes we are healed."

I Peter 2:24

"Who his own self bare our sins in his own body on the tree, that we, being dead to sins, should live unto righteousness: by whose stripes ye were healed."

Defeat of Hindrances

Pray these verses of Scripture for anyone on your prayer list.

Deuteronomy 11:25

"There shall no man be able to stand before you: for the LORD your God shall lay the fear of you and the dread of you upon all the land that ye shall tread upon, as he hath said unto you."

Deuteronomy 33:27

"The eternal God is thy refuge, and underneath are the everlasting arms: and he shall thrust out the enemy from before thee; and shall say, Destroy them."

I Samuel 2:9

"He will keep the feet of his saints, and the wicked shall be silent in darkness; for by strength shall no man prevail."

Psalm 17:8-9

"Keep me as the apple of the eye, hide me under the shadow of thy wings, from the wicked that oppress me, from my deadly enemies, who compass me about."

Psalm 20:1-2

"The LORD hear thee in the day of trouble; the name of the God of Jacob defend thee; send thee help from the sanctuary, and strengthen thee out of Zion."

Psalm 27:5

"For in the time of trouble he shall hide me in his pavilion: in the secret of his tabernacle shall he hide me; he shall set me up upon a rock."

Psalm 32:7

"Thou art my hiding place; thou shalt preserve me from trouble; thou shalt compass me about with songs of deliverance. Selah."

Psalm 37:23-24

"The steps of a good man are ordered by the Lord: and he delighteth in his way. Though he fall, he shall not be utterly cast down: for the Lord upholdeth him with his hand."

Psalm 55:22

"Cast thy burden upon the Lord, and he shall sustain thee: he shall never suffer the righteous to be moved."

Psalm 91:11

"For he shall give his angels charge over thee, to keep thee in all thy ways."

Psalm 91:12

"They shall bear thee up in their hands, lest thou dash thy foot against a stone."

Psalm 119:11

"Thy word have I hid in mine heart, that I might not sin against thee."

Psalm 119:165

"Great peace have they which love thy law: and nothing shall offend them."

Proverbs 4:11-12

"I have taught thee in the way of wisdom; I have led thee in right paths. When thou goest, thy steps shall not be straitened; and when thou runnest, thou shalt not stumble."

I Thessalonians 5:23

"And the very God of peace sanctify you wholly; and I pray God your whole spirit and soul and body be preserved blameless unto the coming of our Lord Jesus Christ."

II Thessalonians 3:3

"But the Lord is faithful, who shall stablish you, and keep you from evil."

Strength for the Journey

"What time I am afraid, I will trust in thee" (Psalm 56:3). At first, this verse of Scripture sounds like a contradiction in terms; fear is the opposite of faith. If you trust, you don't feel fear. Right?

David isn't saying, "I'll never be afraid." He knew his destiny and his anointing, but right then it looked as if it would never come to pass. Hounded by Saul, he fled to the Philistines. They didn't trust him, knowing he had been in Saul's army. He feigned madness and then ran and hid in a cave. This is where we encounter him singing this song:

"What time I am afraid, I will trust in thee. In God I will praise his word, in God I have put my trust; I will not fear what flesh can do unto me" (verses 3-4).

What David was saying is, "There are times when I fear; but when I'm afraid, I know what to do. I will trust in the unfailing Word of God, the sure promises of God."

David, the poet, musician, and prophet, experienced the entire emotional spectrum from times of elation to times of despair, but he had a foundational trust in the Word of God. In our spiritual lives there can be conflict between two areas of our being. In our emotions we may experience fear and perhaps panic.

But there is another area of our being that does not yield to the emotions. In those times, if we have filled our hearts with His Word, from deep within us there comes a confidence. The Spirit will bring to remembrance a promise from God and a peace and confidence that are much deeper than emotions. The words of an old hymn come to mind:

147

There's a deep, settled peace in my soul.
Waves of joy like the sea billows roll.
Every day, every hour, I am kept by His Power.
There's a deep settled peace in my soul.

("Deep Settled Peace," words and music by Kate Peters Sturgill)

Emotions are like waves on the surface, but down deep there is peace! I remember a time from my childhood when we were experiencing a violent thunderstorm with strong winds that shook our tiny house until it felt as if it would lift from the foundation. My mother watched the storm through the windows, and as I hovered close to her and she saw my fear, she would say, "The LORD hath His way in the whirlwind and in the storm, and the clouds are the dust of his feet" (Nahum 1:3b). She reached deep into her spirit to convey confidence to me.

Let us say with David today, "In God I will praise his word, in God I have put my trust."

Read and claim the following verses as promises from God for times when you may be confused, afraid, and spiritually weak or stressed in any way. Personalize them and make them your prayer.

Psalm 61:1-3
"Hear my cry, O God; attend unto my prayer. From the end of the earth will I cry unto thee, when my heart is overwhelmed: lead me to the rock that is higher than I. For thou hast been a shelter for me, and a strong tower from the enemy."

Psalm 62:7-8
"In God is my salvation and my glory: the rock of my strength, and my refuge, is in God. Trust in him at all times; ye people, pour out your heart before him: God is a refuge for us. Selah."

Psalm 94:22

"But the LORD is my defence; and my God is the rock of my refuge."

Isaiah 51:1

"Hearken to me, ye that follow after righteousness, ye that seek the LORD: look unto the rock whence ye are hewn, and to the hole of the pit whence ye are digged."

Psalm 56:3

"What time I am afraid, I will trust in thee."

Psalm 37:23-24

"The steps of a good man are ordered by the LORD: and he delighteth in his way. Though he fall, he shall not be utterly cast down: for the LORD upholdeth him with his hand."

Additional verses that you can pray:

Job 8:20
Psalm 42:11
Psalm 51:10-13
Psalm 55:22
Psalm 71:8-9
Isaiah 41:9-10
Matthew 11:28-30
II Corinthians 4:7-10
Hebrews 10:35-36
I Peter 5:6-8

The Place of Enlargement in Times of Distress

"Hear me when I call, O God of my righteousness:
thou hast enlarged me when I was in distress;
have mercy upon me, and hear my prayer"
(Psalm 4:1).

Many of us have walked through deep valleys. In those times of severe testing of our faith, we are bombarded with the arrows of the enemy of our souls. Satan tries to make us doubt that God loves us and that He truly makes all things work together for our good. Then, when questions arise, he immediately attacks us with guilt for having had even the momentary doubt. He tells us that we have no faith, that it is useless to trust God, and that the sunshine has forever gone from our lives.

It is a truth that the celebratory seasons like Thanksgiving and Christmas can be very difficult for those walking through the valley of grief, disappointment, or disillusionment. It is these times that drive us to God's Word to find sustenance. He is faithful to His covenant and speaks the words that sustain us through the hour of testing and refines our faith, which is more precious to Him than gold. (See I Peter 1:6-7.)

These passages of Scripture help us to realize that He is with us in the fire of the testing of our faith. It is His blessed Spirit that empowers us to continue to trust and believe that the sun will shine again, that we can still be useful in His kingdom.

151

So how do the times of distress bring us to that place of enlargement? Paul explains it in Romans 5:1-5:

> "Therefore being justified by faith, we have peace with God through our Lord Jesus Christ: by whom also we have access by faith into this grace wherein we stand, and rejoice in hope of the glory of God. And not only so, but we glory in tribulations also: knowing that tribulation worketh patience; and patience, experience; and experience, hope; and hope maketh not ashamed; because the love of God is shed abroad in our hearts by the Holy Ghost which is given unto us."

I Peter 5:6-10

> "Humble yourselves therefore under the mighty hand of God, that he may exalt you in due time: casting all your care upon him; for he careth for you. Be sober, be vigilant; because your adversary the devil, as a roaring lion, walketh about, seeking whom he may devour: whom resist stedfast in the faith, knowing that the same afflictions are accomplished in your brethren that are in the world. But the God of all grace, who hath called us unto his eternal glory by Christ Jesus, after that ye have suffered a while, make you perfect, stablish, strengthen, settle you."

Psalm 18:32-36

> "It is God that girdeth me with strength, and maketh my way perfect. He maketh my feet like hinds' feet, and setteth me upon my high places. He teacheh my hands to war, so that a bow of steel is broken by mine arms. Thou hast also given me the shield of thy salvation: and thy right hand hath holden me up, and thy gentleness hath made me great. Thou hast enlarged my steps under me, that my feet did not slip."

Psalm 66: 8-9, 12b

> "O bless our God, ye people, and make the voice of his

praise to be heard: which holdeth our soul in life, and suffereth not our feet to be moved . . . we went through fire and through water: but thou broughtest us out into a wealthy place [a place of enlargement; productivity]."

Additional
Prayer Helps

"And he spake a parable unto them to this end,
that men ought always to pray,
and not to faint"
(Luke 18:1).

"The effectual fervent prayer of a righteous man availeth much"
(James 5:16b).

Focused Prayer for
Each Day of the Week

Sunday - Spiritual Growth

In the name of Jesus Christ I pray . . .

- ❏ Enable me to walk in the spirit of power, love, and self control.
- ❏ Transform me into Your likeness.
- ❏ Teach me to be sensitive to Your voice (spiritual ears and heart).
- ❏ Deepen my hunger for God and the things of God.
- ❏ Give me wisdom and knowledge as I read Your precious Word.
- ❏ Give me the strength to withstand all trials.
- ❏ Help me to become a virtuous woman of God.

Monday - Relationships

In the name of Jesus Christ I pray . . .

- ❏ Make me into a godly role model.
- ❏ Use me to touch the lives of others.
- ❏ Empower me with boldness to speak Your Word.
- ❏ Place a desire in my heart to become a soulwinner.
- ❏ Give me discernment when helping others.
- ❏ Help me to be sensitive to the needs of those around me.
- ❏ Guide me to find the right prayer partner (soul mate).

Tuesday - Direction
In the name of Jesus Christ I pray . . .

- ❑ I seek Your wisdom, Lord, and not the wisdom of the world.
- ❑ Give me personal direction and vision.
- ❑ Help me to be obedient to Your calling in my life.
- ❑ Direct me away from bad influences in my life.
- ❑ May I be led by Your Holy Spirit and not by fleshly desires.
- ❑ When I go astray, help me to get back on the right track.
- ❑ I give you my life; lead me, guide me, and direct my steps.

Wednesday - Physical, Emotional, and Spiritual Wellbeing
In the name of Jesus Christ I pray . . .

- ❑ Place a desire in my heart to take proper care of my body.
- ❑ Teach me to eat healthy and to choose nutritious foods.
- ❑ Protect me from accidents, diseases, injury, or any physical, mental, or emotional abuse.
- ❑ Bless me with a sound mind.
- ❑ Plant the fruit of Your Spirit in me and cause it to grow.
- ❑ Bless me with wisdom, discernment, and guidance.
- ❑ Encourage me to seek You each day for my Daily Bread.

Thursday - Spiritual Warfare
In the name of Jesus Christ I pray . . .

- ❑ Train me to become a mighty prayer warrior.
- ❑ I put on the full armor of God.
- ❑ I bind all powers of darkness in the name of Jesus Christ.
- ❑ Reveal the strongholds in my life and deliver me from all evil.
- ❑ I claim that no weapon formed against me will prosper.
- ❑ Free me from things that bind, hold, or separate me from You.
- ❑ Give me boldness in the Holy Ghost.

Friday - Priorities

In the name of Jesus Christ I pray . . .

- ❏ Set my priorities in perfect order.
- ❏ Help me to find time to spend alone with You.
- ❏ Help me to cling to what is good and keep myself pure and holy.
- ❏ Help me to become spiritually-minded, not carnally-minded.
- ❏ Show me the importance of being grounded in Your Word.
- ❏ May my priorities line up with Your priorities for my life.
- ❏ Be ruler over my heart. Don't let anything separate me from You.

Saturday - Family

In the name of Jesus Christ I pray . . .

- ❏ Keep my family in the center of Your will.
- ❏ Open the lines of communication in my family.
- ❏ Fill my home with peace and unity.
- ❏ Bind my family together with Your love.
- ❏ Teach me to train up my children in the way they should go.
- ❏ I declare salvation to each family member in Jesus' name.
- ❏ Help couples to be able to work out their differences.

Overcome Prayer Fatigue with Prayer Walking

Have you ever experienced "prayer fatigue"? When prayer fatigue sets in, change your mode of prayer. Try doing more worship than agonizing prayer for awhile. None of us are able to endure strong prayer incessantly. Our body, soul, and spirit needs refreshing. Try a prayer drive, alone or with someone, blessing the homes and the inhabitants of your city or region as you go.

Park in the vicinity of taverns and liquor stores and observe the clientele. Let empathy sweep over your heart for these individuals and try to imagine how families are robbed of God's best by the demon of alcohol. Take authority over the power of alcohol as these men, women, and youth come and go.

Drive to a park and as you circle it, pray over the children and parents, many of whom are single. Try to imagine how devastating their divorce may have been and let the Holy Spirit flow through you as you pray.

Move to the business district and industrial parks, asking God to bless these entrepreneurs that they in turn might bless the community with jobs. Drive around schools and pray for the students and teachers. Bless that school in the name of Jesus Christ and take authority over substance and alcohol abuse and immorality, which rules and ruins the lives of many youth.

The Old Testament has many passages relating to walking an area for God's glory. Joshua taking the city of Jericho (Joshua 6) is probably the most familiar account of the powerful act of walking and praying. It is a model of extending God's kingdom through

161

man's humble availability and faith joined by God's miraculous ability. Our prayers can be a means of releasing God's power to cause the walls of unbelief, violence, and evil to come down.

Although this passage does not indicate walking and praying through our city, there is probably no better way to cover a community with prayer than to walk and pray through its neighborhoods. The Bible offers many models of effective ways to pray. "Prayer walking," as a term, is never mentioned in Scripture, but Jesus prayerfully looked over the city of Jerusalem. Consider the following verses.

Genesis 13:17

"Arise, walk through the land in the length of it and in the breadth of it; for I will give it unto thee."

Joshua 1:3

"Every place that the sole of your foot shall tread upon, that have I given unto you."

Jeremiah 29:7

"And seek the peace of the city whither I have caused you to be carried away captives, and pray unto the LORD for it: for in the peace thereof shall ye have peace."

Matthew 23:37

"O Jerusalem, Jerusalem, thou that killest the prophets, and stonest them which are sent unto thee, how often would I have gathered thy children together, even as a hen gathereth her chickens under her wings, and ye would not!"

Acts 17:16

"Now while Paul waited for them at Athens, his spirit was stirred in him, when he saw the city wholly given to idolatry."

God Is Still
on the Throne!

In Psalm 11:3, David asks a question: "If the foundations be destroyed, what can the righteous do?" Many of us are asking that same question today. In my lifetime, I have observed the erosion of a once God-fearing nation into a secular society. The Christian worldview is increasingly no longer welcome in the public forum of discussion and debate.

Isaiah wrote of a time in Israel when "judgment is turned away backward, and justice standeth afar off: for truth is fallen in the street, and equity cannot enter. Yea, truth faileth; and he that departeth from evil maketh himself a prey: and the LORD saw it, and it displeased him that there was no judgment. And he saw that there was no man, and wondered that there was no intercessor" (Isaiah 59:14-16a).

Then Ezekiel wrote of the national sin of his time and God's desires: "And I sought for a man among them, that should make up the hedge, and stand in the gap before me for the land, that I should not destroy it: but I found none" (Ezekiel 22:30).

Back to the original question, "What can the righteous do?" The answer is in the following verse of Scripture: "The LORD is in his holy temple, the LORD's throne is in heaven" (Psalm 11:4).

The same throne that Isaiah saw in his time of despair (chapter 6) is still there today. The promises are there for those who seek God. God still hears those who "stand in the gap" so today, let's earnestly seek God for repentance, reformation, revival, and restoration in our nation. Let's plead the power of the blood and name of Jesus, the risen, victorious Lord, over our land for protection against terrorism.

> "*I exhort therefore, that, first of all, supplications, prayers, intercessions, and giving of thanks, be made for all men; for kings, and for all that are in authority; that we may lead a quiet and peaceable life in all godliness and honesty. For this is good and acceptable in the sight of God our Saviour; who will have all men to be saved, and to come unto the knowledge of the truth*" (I Timothy 2:1-4).

God is still on His throne!

Books Available from
More to Life

Alive in Him: Learning to Live Abundantly in Christ—A study for all ages that walks one through repentance, the new birth, and how to live for God. Wonderful for new converts, for Sunday school, for Bible study, and especially helpful for prison ministry.

More to Life Bible Study Series
- *Finding God's Favor*
- *Pursuing God's Plan*
- *Walking God's Way*

This series of studies is a proven, effective tool for reaching friends, family, co-workers, and others with a greater understanding of God's plan of salvation. It is also an excellent tool for small group ladies studies. Four lessons per book.

Parents and Daughters Talk—This book is designed to open dialogue with your daughter and give her experiences and permission to exercise decision-making skills. We must provide our daughters with not only technical/medical information, but also with the mind and voice to take the facts and make the right choices for her whole person, her whole life.

Parents and Sons Talk—Designed to help mothers and fathers consider the issues facing young men growing up in an increasingly violent, promiscuous world. Remember, if parents don't talk to their sons, somebody will.

Praying the Word Effectively—Promises for all occasions in life are found throughout Scripture. This selection of verses will awaken your desire to search for more of God's promises. Learn to pray the Word and be effective in your prayers for all of life's situations.

The Girl in the Dress: Uncovering the Mystery of Modesty—This book, written in an easy-to-read style, provides practical insights and scriptural references that explore biblical modesty. As we live and dress according to the Word of God, our inner beauty will take over and the outward result will be one that makes us truly beautiful. For all ages.

The Good Life—Success is measured in so many ways—fame, wealth, power—and today's young women want it all. This study defines success through the Word of God. This is an excellent witnessing tool and also great for personal study for pre-teen and teen girls.

This is Life and I Need Answers
This is Life and I Need More Answers
These two books are written in a heart-to-heart style by ordinary women who have triumphed over some of life's toughest situations. Each book contains nineteen chapters that focus on critical issues women face today. These are excellent resources for personal enrichment or small group discussion. It is also very helpful for pastors and counselors.

These books are available through Ladies Ministries.
For discount prices on quantity orders
call 314-837-7304 Ext. 412 and ask for Jane Buford.

To be assured of Bible-based literature, always look for these registered trademarks:

More to Life
THROUGH GOD'S WORD